I first saw a fancifully decorated cake—a coconut-covered bunny—at my sister's Girl Scout badge ceremony and, with all the other ten-year-olds in the room, couldn't keep my mind on anything but the promise of a slice. I've never forgotten that experience; it resonates today, reminding me that celebrations are so important for their memories and simple joys.

That is what this book is all about—creating whimsical, charming cakes that will bring smiles of awe and anticipation to the children in your life, and leave lasting memories. Whether you're a novice cake decorator or an ace, whether you bake from scratch, from a mix, or start with a ready-made cake, we invite you to begin your party by selecting a cake with the perfect theme—rocket ship or robot, kitty cupcakes or an edible rainbow—and begin making memories as you arrange and embellish the pieces.

The thirty-five cakes on the following pages are meant to inspire and delight; mix up the colors and decorations to make them your own—and don't forget your camera!

—Matthew Mead

Guidelines for Baking, Assembling, and Decorating

CAKES FOR KIDS

CAKES FOR KIDS

**35 Colorful Cakes with Easy-to-Follow Tips & Techniques
by Matthew Mead**

CHRONICLE BOOKS

SAN FRANCISCO

The author wishes to thank everyone who contributed to this project, especially my wife, Jenny, who took such beautiful photographs. My assistants, Lisa Renauld and Lisa Bisson, worked tirelessly on the decorations for each cake, and Sue Chandler and Mandy Foss did even more specialty decorating and baking. Thanks, too, to Carol Spier, who always knows what to say and how to say it. Everyone at Downtown Bookworks, especially Pam Abrams, Julie Merberg, and Sara Newberry, and all the editors at Chronicle Books deserve my deep appreciation. Lastly, to that child inside of all of us who eagerly awaits that first piece of cake. —Matthew Mead

Produced by Downtown Bookworks Inc.
President: Julie Merberg
Senior Vice President: Pam Abrams
Instructions: Carol Spier
Illustrations: Laura Hartman Maestro

Library of Congress Cataloging-in-Publication Data available.

ISBN 978-0-8118-6190-8

Manufactured in Singapore.

10 9 8 7 6 5 4 3 2 1

Chronicle Books LLC
680 Second Street
San Francisco, California 94107

www.chroniclebooks.com

Contents

COOL TOOLS FOR CAKES

To make any of these cakes, have basic baking supplies on hand: a variety of bowls, whisks, spoons, and rubber and metal spatulas. A rolling pin is handy for crushing toppings and rolling fondant. Specific cake pans are indicated with each project. Use a long serrated knife (at least 9 inches) to cut the cakes as required.

Offset spatulas: These palette knife–type tools have an offset blade, which provides control and leverage when moving or icing a cake, and they are key for frosting and lifting. The smaller sizes are good for frosting small or tight areas, and the larger ones for frosting large areas and also for lifting frosted cakes from work space to serving platter. You need at least two, one with a 4½-inch-long blade and another with a 10-inch-long blade.

Decorating bags and assorted tips are essential for piped embellishments. The size and type of tip is specified in each of the recipe equipment lists. The disposable clear plastic decorating bags work just as well as the cloth ones. There is a coupler system available in baking supply stores and cake decorating sections of craft stores. To use couplers, place the channeled screw-top piece inside the pastry bag, then fill the bag with icing. Place the tip on the outside of the coupler and screw the top piece over the tip and onto the coupler. This makes it easy to change tips without having to start a new pastry bag.

Tweezers, wooden skewers, and small spoons are invaluable for arranging decorations. Use wooden toothpicks to mark designs onto cake tops or frosting.

BAKING YOUR CAKE OR CUPCAKES

When you have multiple pans in the oven, plan to turn them 180° halfway through the baking time. Adjust your baking time by adding 5 to 7 minutes to account for having the oven door open and the additional demand on the oven.

The recipes in this book make more batter than is required for many of the projects (step 1 of each project alerts you when this is so). Unless indicated otherwise, we assume all cake pans are 2 inches deep and expect you to fill them two-thirds full, and then bake the excess batter separately. If your project calls for more than one pan, it's important that all the pans be filled to the same depth so the adjacent cake layers will be the same thickness.

If you begin with a boxed cake mix, follow the package directions for mixing and baking. If your project calls for more than one pan, be sure to fill each to the same depth. You may have a different amount of batter from that specified in our recipes.

To get off to a good start, be sure you prepare the cake pans as indicated in your recipe. A range of baking times is given for each pan size; check for doneness when the first time specified has elapsed.

To remove a cake from its pan after it has cooled for 10 minutes, invert a wire rack over the cake in the pan, invert them together so the cake drops onto the rack, and lift off the pan. Peel off any waxed paper. Invert a second wire rack on top of the cake. Gently invert both racks with the cake in between, and then remove the first rack so that the cake is right side up.

To freeze a cake before decorating, wrap the completely cooled layers individually in plastic wrap and freeze. Let them thaw for 1 to 2 hours before frosting. A chilled cake surface has fewer crumbs—making it easier to frost—so it's a fine idea to do the baking ahead of time and freeze the cooled cake.

CUTTING & ASSEMBLING

To prepare a cake for frosting, level the domed top that naturally occurs during baking. Before cutting, insert toothpicks around the edge for a guide; slice right below them. Use a long serrated knife to slice off the dome. However, if you want your project to have a domed top and plan to contour it with frosting, skip this step.

To cut a cooled cake in order to configure the pieces of a project, place the cake on a cutting board. Use a toothpick to prick the outline of any pattern pieces into the cake top, or measure with a ruler and prick the key points for cutting. Use a serrated knife (9 inches is usually a good length) and guide straight cuts with a straightedge ruler.

To use a parchment paper pattern for cutting and decorating: The projects for which you'll need to mark complex shapes for cutting or decorating include diagrams with dimensions to guide you when you are prepping the cake. You may find it easier to mark these shapes if you make a parchment paper pattern for them. A transparent, gridded ruler is handy for keeping things square while you draft the pattern according to the diagram.

There are two ways to use a parchment paper pattern: Cut it out and mark around it, or leave it whole and mark through it. In either case, use a toothpick or a skewer to prick the outline of the design into the cake top or frosting. If you leave the pattern whole, the relative position of the design elements will be maintained when you put it on the cake.

To bond adjacent pieces when assembling a cake, spread frosting between them. On vertical seams, use a thin layer of frosting so the dimension does not change too much. On horizontal seams, you can use a thicker layer of frosting.

Ready-made candy flowers are sweet options too.

FROSTING AND DECORATING

READY-MADE FROSTINGS

Several types of ready-to-use icings are available. Below are the ones most frequently used for the recipes in this book.

Decorating icing comes in 4.25-ounce tubes in a range of colors. You'll find piping tips specially made to fit these tubes wherever they are sold. Use decorating icing to create embellishments when you need only a small amount of a specific color.

Fondant is a pliable icing that can be sculpted, draped, or rolled and cut into shapes (or rolled, cut, and then sculpted). It comes in colors or can be tinted. It holds its shape when it dries.

Cookie icing comes in 10-ounce bottles in white; it is similar to homemade Royal Icing (page 20). When it dries, it is very hard and shiny and can be tinted. Use it whenever you want embellishments or as a gravity-defying edible cement—it's especially good for adhering decorations to the side of a cake.

Icing writers, available in limited colors, come in 3-ounce tubes with a round tip attached. Use them to draw fine details on your project.

FOOD COLORING

Choose your colors: The best food colorings to use are the gel and paste varieties; the liquid type comes in fewer colors and you need much more of it than of the gel or paste to achieve the same tint intensity. If you wish to mix a custom color, mix gel with gel, paste with paste, or liquid with liquid.

Gel color comes in a bottle with a squeeze top; simply squeeze out drops of color.

Paste color comes in a small jar; it is more concentrated than gel and you need less of it. Use a toothpick or the tip of an offset spatula to add a "drop" of paste color to your frosting.

To tint frosting, add a few drops of color, mix thoroughly, and then add and mix in more color one drop at a time until the desired intensity is achieved.

FROSTING AND PIPING 101

- *Apply frosting in two coats* to the top and sides of an assembled cake. The first coat should be thin, just enough to seal the surface from loose crumbs. Apply the first coat and then refrigerate the cake for 1 hour or place it in the freezer for ½ hour. Remove the cake from the refrigerator and apply a second, thicker coat of frosting.

- *To handle frosted cake pieces* in order to assemble them for a project, use a small spatula to support the piece and guide it lightly with your fingers; touch up the frosting after positioning the piece. You can leave some areas unfrosted and then complete the frosting after the piece is positioned.

- *To prevent frosting* from hardening between decorating steps, cover it with damp paper towels or plastic wrap.

- *To store frosting for a later use,* refrigerate it in a covered, airtight container for 2 to 3 days.

- *Always clean stray frosting from the serving plate* before adding other decorations—scrape it off with a spatula or wipe with a paper towel.

- *Practice unfamiliar techniques* on waxed paper to become comfortable using them.

- *To fill a pastry bag with frosting or glaze,* first fit a coupler and tip on the bag. Then fold down about 2 inches at the open end. Grasp the bag below the folded-down section (or support it in a small glass) and fill the bag half full with the frosting. Unfold the bag and twist the top, forcing the frosting down into the tip.

- *To pipe an outline,* hold the tip at a 45-degree angle close to the cake. Squeeze the bag with even pressure and move the tip to outline the design. When done with a line, stop the pressure, touch the tip to the surface, and then lift it.

- *To fill an outlined area neatly with frosting,* pipe on some frosting and spread it with a spatula.

- *To fill an outlined area neatly with glaze,* pipe on a thin layer of glaze; spread it with a spatula if the area is large.

- *To achieve a very smooth surface,* dip a spatula in hot water, wipe it dry, and pass it over the applied frosting. Dip it in warm water to smooth glaze.

Hold the decorating bag at a 45-degree angle to the cake and squeeze out the frosting while moving your hand in whatever pattern is required—for example, outlining spots to be filled with a topping.

ADDING SUGARS, SPRINKLES, & OTHER EDIBLE TOPPINGS

Search any cake-decorations supplier and you'll find a wealth of edible products to sprinkle on top of your confections. Finishes range from sparkling to lustrous to matte, and shapes vary from fine dusts and coarse glitters to spherical dragées, nonpareils, and cylindrical jimmies, as well as small hearts, flowers, and assorted flat geometrics. Crushed cookies (put them in a sealable plastic bag and crush with a rolling pin) and shredded coconut are other options that add tasty texture.

To position small decorations, use your fingers or long tweezers. Adhere the decoration with a dab of icing as instructed in the project; pipe the icing onto the back of the decoration or dot it on with a skewer.

To sprinkle toppings, use a small spoon and work slowly to scatter the topping over the surface; don't overfill the spoon. You can use a skewer to push the topping into narrow areas of a design.

To keep from marring your work, arrange decorations from left to right if you are right-handed, or from right to left if you are left-handed. It is generally easiest to arrange a concentric pattern if you work from the perimeter toward the center, rotating the cake as you go so you don't disturb your work.

DISPLAYING & SERVING

The dimensions at the beginning of each project provide a minimum size for the base or platter you'll need for the finished cake. Refer to the project photo to see how the cake is displayed and decide if you want the platter to be large enough to hold additional embellishments.

For ease of handling, put the cake on a cardboard base of the same shape before you decorate it and then transfer the decorated cake on this base to the serving platter. Round and rectangular cardboard bases in assorted sizes can be purchased in the cake decorations section of crafts supply stores. If your cake shape is other than round or rectangular or you can't find a base the right size, buy one larger than you need. Place the undecorated cake on the base and draw around it, leaving a margin of about ¼ inch. (For a single-layer cake composed of several cut shapes, arrange the pieces on the base but do not bond them with frosting; leave a larger margin, depending on the number of seams, to accommodate the bonding, which makes the overall pattern larger.) Remove the cake and cut the base on the drawn line using a craft knife. Place the cake back on the base and then decorate it.

To transfer a frosted or decorated cake to a serving platter, slide a large spatula under the cardboard base; lift the base and place your free hand under it. Put the spatula aside and put your other hand under the base. Transfer the cake on the base to the platter.

If you don't have a large platter, display the cake on a pastry board, a sturdy piece of cardboard, or a strong box lid. Cover the board with foil or colorful paper. If you are not using a cardboard base of the same shape as the cake, place waxed paper or plastic food wrap under the cake before decorating if the serving board is not covered with a food-safe material.

PROTECTING A FINISHED CAKE

If you wish, purchase a fold-up cardboard cake-storage box to protect your cake until ready to serve. These are like the gift boxes you assemble by sliding tabs into slots. Make sure the box is sufficiently larger than your cake.

BAKING TIMES

Use this guide to judge baking times for different-sized pans. Fill muffin cups and all other 2-inch-deep pans two-thirds full; if there is surplus batter, bake it in another appropriate pan. Preheat the oven to 350 °F (unless otherwise specified below). Oven type, pan quality, and atmospheric conditions may affect the baking time, so check for doneness when the first time in the specified range has elapsed. A cake is done when a toothpick inserted in its center comes out clean.

350 °F

PAN	BAKING TIME
4-inch round	20 to 25 minutes
5-inch round	20 to 25 minutes
6-inch round	20 to 25 minutes
8-inch square or round	30 to 35 minutes
9-inch square or round	30 to 35 minutes
10-inch square or round	30 to 35 minutes
12-inch square or round	30 to 35 minutes
9-by-13-inch rectangle	35 to 40 minutes
12-by-16-inch rectangle	50 to 60 minutes*
9-inch heart	30 to 35 minutes
10-inch heart	30 to 35 minutes
12-inch heart	35 to 40 minutes
9-inch Bundt or ring pan	20 to 30 minutes
10-inch Bundt or ring pan	20 to 30 minutes
6-inch half-sphere	30 minutes
Mini muffin cups	6 to 8 minutes
Standard muffin cups	10 to 12 minutes
Jumbo muffin cups	12 to 15 minutes

*at 335 °F

BASIC RECIPES

CHOCOLATE CAKE

This recipe makes a standard 8-inch or 9-inch 2-layer cake, enough to serve 12 to 16 or 24 cupcakes.

EQUIPMENT

Cake pans, as needed

Waxed or parchment paper

Paper cupcake liners (if making cupcakes)

Medium bowl

Whisk

Electric mixer

Rubber spatula

Toothpick

Wire cooling racks

Shortening, as needed

2 cups all-purpose flour, plus extra for the pans

¾ cup unsweetened cocoa powder

1 teaspoon baking soda

¾ teaspoon baking powder

½ teaspoon salt

¾ cup (6 ounces) unsalted butter, at room temperature

2 cups sugar

3 large eggs, at room temperature

2 teaspoons vanilla extract

1½ cups whole milk

1. Preheat the oven to 350 °F.

2. Read the directions for your chosen decorated cake to see what size pans to use. Lightly grease the bottom of each cake pan, then line it with waxed paper or parchment paper and grease and lightly flour the bottom and sides. If you are making cupcakes, line the cups with paper liners.

3. In a medium bowl, whisk together the 2 cups flour, the cocoa powder, baking soda, baking powder, and salt.

4. Using an electric mixer on medium to high speed, beat the butter in a large bowl for 30 seconds. With the mixer on medium speed, gradually add the sugar, about ¼ cup at a time, beating each addition 3 to 4 minutes or until well combined. Using a rubber spatula, scrape down the sides of the bowl; continue beating on medium speed for 2 minutes more, until the mixture is smooth and creamy. Add the eggs 1 at a time, beating for 30 seconds after each addition. Beat in the vanilla extract.

5. With the mixer on low speed and beating until just combined after each addition, beat the flour mixture into the butter mixture in 3 additions, alternating with 2 additions of the milk. With the mixer on medium to high speed, beat the batter for 20 seconds more.

6. Using a rubber spatula, spread the batter in the prepared pans. Unless your project directions indicate otherwise, fill round, square, rectangular, or shaped pans two-thirds full; fill cupcake cups two-thirds full. Bake the cake(s), referring to your project or the chart on page 15 for the baking time; each cake is done when a toothpick inserted in the center comes out clean. If there is excess batter, spread it in a prepared appropriate-size pan and bake it as indicated on the chart.

7. Transfer the cake in the pan to a wire rack. Cool in the pan for 10 minutes, then invert onto the rack, lift off the pan, and peel off the waxed paper. Let the cake cool completely on the rack. Remove cupcakes from the pans after cooling for 15 minutes.

DEVIL'S FOOD CAKE VARIATION
Follow the chocolate cake recipe, using 1¼ teaspoons baking soda and omitting the baking powder.

YELLOW CAKE

This recipe makes a standard 8-inch or 9-inch 2-layer cake, enough to serve 12 to 16, or 24 cupcakes.

EQUIPMENT

Cake pans, as needed

Waxed or parchment paper

Paper cupcake liners (if making cupcakes)

Medium bowl

Whisk

Electric mixer

Rubber spatula

Toothpick

Wire cooling racks

Shortening, as needed

2 ½ cups all-purpose flour, plus extra for pans

2 ½ teaspoons baking powder

½ teaspoon salt

⅔ cup (5 ⅔ ounces) unsalted butter or margarine, at room temperature

1 ¾ cups sugar

2 large eggs, at room temperature

1 ½ teaspoons vanilla extract

1 ¼ cups milk

2 teaspoons grated fresh orange zest or lemon zest

1. Preheat the oven to 350 °F.

2. Read the directions for your chosen decorated cake to see what size pans to use. Lightly grease the bottom of each cake pan, then line it with waxed paper or parchment paper and grease and lightly flour the bottom and sides. If you are making cupcakes, line the cups with paper liners.

3. In a medium bowl, whisk together the 2 ½ cups flour, the baking powder, and salt.

4. Using an electric mixer on medium to high speed, beat the butter in a large bowl for 30 seconds. With the mixer on medium speed, gradually add the sugar, about ¼ cup at a time, beating each addition 3 to 4 minutes or until well combined. Using a rubber spatula, scrape down the sides of the bowl; continue beating on medium speed for 2 minutes more, until the mixture is smooth and creamy. Add the eggs 1 at a time, beating for 30 seconds after each addition. Beat in the vanilla extract.

5. With the mixer on low speed and beating until just combined after each addition, beat the flour mixture into the butter mixture in 3 additions, alternating with 2 additions of the milk. Add the orange zest and, with the mixer on medium to high speed, beat the batter for 20 seconds more.

6. Using a rubber spatula, spread the batter in the prepared pans. Unless your project directions indicate otherwise, fill round, square, rectangular, or shaped pans two-thirds full; fill cupcake cups two-thirds full. Bake the cake(s), referring to your project or the chart on page 15 for the baking time; each cake is done when a wooden toothpick inserted in the center comes out clean. If there is excess batter, spread it in a prepared appropriate-size pan and bake it as indicated on the chart.

7. Transfer the cake in the pan to a wire rack. Cool in the pan for 10 minutes, then invert onto the rack, lift off the pan, and peel off the waxed paper. Let the cake cool completely on the rack. Remove cupcakes from the pans after cooling for 15 minutes.

MARBLE CAKE

This recipe makes a standard 8-inch or 9-inch 2-layer cake, enough to serve 12 to 16, or 24 cupcakes.

EQUIPMENT

Cake pans, as needed

Waxed or parchment paper

Paper cupcake liners (if making cupcakes)

Medium bowl

Whisk

Electric mixer

Rubber spatula

Spoon

Toothpick

Wire cooling racks

Shortening, as needed

2 cups all-purpose flour, plus extra for pans

1 1/2 teaspoons baking powder

1/2 teaspoon baking soda

1/4 teaspoon salt

3/4 cup (6 ounces) unsalted butter or margarine, at room temperature

1 1/4 cups sugar

2 large eggs, at room temperature

2 teaspoons vanilla extract

1 cup milk

1/3 cup chocolate-flavored syrup

1. Preheat the oven to 350 °F.

2. Read the directions for your chosen decorated cake to see what size pans to use. Lightly grease the bottom of each cake pan, then line it with waxed paper or parchment paper and grease and lightly flour the bottom and sides. If you are making cupcakes, line the cups with paper liners.

3. In a medium bowl, whisk together the 2 cups flour, the baking powder, baking soda, and salt.

4. Using an electric mixer on medium to high speed, beat the butter in a large bowl for 30 seconds. With the mixer on medium speed, gradually add the sugar, about 1/4 cup at a time, beating each addition 3 to 4 minutes or until well combined. Using a rubber spatula, scrape down the sides of the bowl; continue beating on medium speed for 2 minutes more, until the mixture is smooth and creamy. Add the eggs 1 at a time, beating for 30 seconds after each addition. Beat in the vanilla extract.

5. With the mixer on low speed and beating until just combined after each addition, beat the flour mixture into the butter mixture in 3 additions, alternating with 2 additions of the milk. With the mixer on medium to high speed, beat the batter for 20 seconds more.

6. Transfer 1 1/2 cups of the batter to a small bowl or 2-cup measuring cup. Stir in the chocolate-flavored syrup.

7. Using a rubber spatula, spread the light-colored batter in the prepared pan. Unless your project directions indicate otherwise, fill round, square, rectangular, or shaped pans two-thirds full; fill cupcake cups two-thirds full. Spoon the dark batter on top of the light batter, dropping it at random intervals over the surface (drop just 1 spoonful on each cupcake). Holding the spatula vertically, gently cut through the batters in a swirling pattern (use a skewer to marble cupcakes).

8. Bake the cake(s), referring to your project or the chart on page 15 for the baking time; each cake is done when a toothpick inserted in the center comes out clean. If there is excess batter, spread it in a prepared appropriate-size pan and bake it as indicated on the chart.

9. Transfer the cake in the pan to a wire rack. Cool in the pan for 10 minutes, then invert onto the rack, lift off the pan, and peel off the waxed paper. Let the cake cool completely on the rack. Remove cupcakes from the pans after cooling for 15 minutes.

CLASSIC ICING GLAZE

Tint this glaze any color you like, and use it to adhere candy sprinkles, coconut, crushed cookies, or similar sprinkled decorations to a cake. Apply the glaze to the cake with a teaspoon, then use an offset spatula dipped in warm water to spread it. Apply the sprinkles immediately. The glaze may also be placed in a decorating bag and piped onto a cake to outline a design.

MAKES 2 CUPS

EQUIPMENT
Large bowl
Wooden spoon

24 ounces (3 cups) confectioners'
sugar, sifted
¼ cup plus 2 teaspoons light-
colored corn syrup
1 tablespoon water

1. In a large bowl, add the corn syrup to the sugar; stir with a wooden spoon until combined. Stir in the water. The glaze should be thick but pour-able and spreadable. If it is too thick, stir in more water, a few drops at a time. Refrigerate in an airtight container for up to 3 days.

ROYAL ICING

This is the classic icing to use when you want to "paint" the decoration on a cake or cookies. It dries very hard and is good for securing and supporting decorations.

MAKES 3 CUPS

EQUIPMENT
Medium bowl
Whisk
Electric mixer

1 pound (1 box) confectioners'
sugar, sifted (4 ½ cups)
3 tablespoons meringue powder
(see Resources, page 128)
½ teaspoon cream of tartar
½ cup warm water
1 teaspoon vanilla extract

1. In a medium bowl, whisk together the confectioners' sugar, meringue powder, and cream of tartar. Add the water and vanilla extract; beat with an electric mixer on low speed until combined. Beat on high speed for 7 to 10 minutes, or until the mixture is very stiff. Refrigerate in an airtight container for 2 to 3 days.

CREAMY WHITE FROSTING

This frosting has a thick consistency that is easy to work with—you can contour it or add texture to it. Also, you can patch it if it becomes marred while you're arranging a cake. The recipe makes enough frosting to cover the tops and sides of two 8-inch or 9-inch cake layers. For a single-layer 9-by-13-inch cake, make just half the recipe.

Shortening has a simpler taste than butter, with a melting point of 106 °F. Butter melts somewhere between 88 °F and 98 °F, depending on the amount of fat in the brand. You can see that if you need to serve a pure buttercream-decorated cake on a hot day, you could have melted decorations and a less than desirable cake. Shortening yields a soft but durable frosting that can be molded with your hands.

MAKES ABOUT 3 CUPS

EQUIPMENT

Electric mixer

1 cup vegetable shortening

1½ teaspoons vanilla extract

½ teaspoon lemon extract, orange extract, or almond extract

1 pound (1 box) confectioners' sugar, sifted (4½ cups)

3 to 4 tablespoons milk

1. With a mixer on medium speed, beat together the shortening, vanilla extract, and lemon extract in a medium bowl for 30 seconds.

2. Slowly add half the confectioners' sugar, beating well. Beat in 2 tablespoons of the milk. Gradually beat in the remaining powdered sugar and enough of the remaining milk until the icing reaches a spreadable consistency. Store in an airtight container in the refrigerator for 2 or 3 days.

SEVEN-MINUTE FROSTING

This frosting is perishable, so make it the day you plan to serve the cake and refrigerate any leftovers after the party. The recipe makes enough frosting to cover the tops and sides of two 8-inch or 9-inch cake layers or one 10-inch tube cake, with some extra.

MAKES 4 CUPS

EQUIPMENT

Double boiler

Electric mixer

Spoon or rubber spatula

1½ cups sugar

⅓ cup cold water

2 egg whites

¼ teaspoon cream of tartar or 2 teaspoons light-colored corn syrup

1 teaspoon vanilla extract

1. Combine the sugar, water, egg whites, and cream of tartar in the top of a double boiler. Using an electric mixer on low speed, beat the ingredients for 30 seconds to combine.

2. Boil a small amount of water in the bottom of the double boiler. Place the top of the double boiler, with the frosting ingredients, on top. Cook the frosting on medium heat, beating constantly with the mixer on high speed, for about 7 minutes, or until the frosting forms stiff peaks when the beaters are lifted. Remove the top of the double boiler from the bottom and, using a spoon or rubber spatula, stir in the vanilla extract. Beat the frosting for 2 to 3 minutes more, or until it is spreadable. Allow the frosting to cool; it should be slightly warm or at room temperature when you use it. Discard any leftovers. Store frosted cake in a cool, dry place until ready to serve.

The cakes and cupcakes in this section are considered easy—
but no one besides you needs to know that. These projects
are so clever and unique, they're sure to impress. Any of them
can be made with our basic recipes (see pages 16 to 21)—or
a store-bought mix to save more time. To make party day
as relaxed as possible, I like to bake the day before I ice and
decorate. Just be sure to cool cakes completely before wrapping and storing them in a cool, dry place.

If you're serving a crowd of kids—like a school party where you
need to supply the whole class—check out the four different
cupcake ideas in this section (pages 29, 35, 47, and 51). Not
only are they delightful, but they're simple enough for children
to help with the decorations. That's true of many of these
cakes. One mom who baked the Over the Rainbow cake (page
59) told me that her daughter sorted bagfuls of M&M's by
color, then helped place them in a beautiful arc on the cake.
Whether you're making a cake together or creating a surprise,
the projects here fit the bill for busy bakers.

projects

SWEET HEART

If pink won't please, choose your child's favorite colors for the frosting and candy trimmings. For Valentine's Day, go with red frosting and red and pink rock candy, and finish with conversation heart candies and nonpareil sprinkles.

SERVES 12 TO 16
MAKES ONE 10-INCH HEART

EQUIPMENT

Two flat-bottomed 10-inch heart pans

Waxed or parchment paper

Toothpick

Wire cooling racks

12-inch round cake plate or cardboard base (see page 14), for serving

Small offset spatula

Resealable plastic bag

Hammer or rolling pin

Small spoon

1 tablespoon shortening

2 tablespoons flour

1 recipe Marble Cake batter (page 18)

2 recipes Creamy White Frosting (page 21), tinted pink

About 10 rock candy sticks, mix of pink and purple

Dragées (4 mm size), mix of pink, blue, yellow, green, and silver, for sprinkling

Purple food glitter, for dusting

1. Preheat the oven to 350 °F. Lightly grease the bottom of each cake pan, then line it with waxed paper or parchment paper and grease and lightly flour the bottom and sides. Fill the prepared pans two-thirds full with the cake batter and bake the cakes until a toothpick inserted into the center of the cake comes out clean, 30 to 35 minutes. Cool the cakes completely in the pans on cooling racks and then turn them out onto the racks.

2. Place 1 cooled cake layer on the cake plate. Using an offset spatula, spread ¾ cup of the frosting over the top. Place the second layer on top of the first, aligning the edges. Spread the remaining frosting over the top and sides of the cake.

3. To break the rock candy into chunks, place the sticks in a resealable plastic bag on a work surface and tap with a hammer or rolling pin.

4. Arrange pieces of the rock candy along the top edge and around the bottom edge of the cake.

5. Sprinkle the dragées over the top of the cake with a small spoon. If necessary, press the dragées into the frosting with a skewer. Sprinkle a few dragées on the plate.

6. Sprinkle the food glitter over the cake. Store the cake in a cool, dry place for up to 2 days. Cover the sliced cake with plastic wrap.

To easily achieve
a mix of dragée colors
when you sprinkle,
first mix them together
in a small dish.

HOST OF GHOSTS

Super fast and not at all scary—these whimsical ghosts gather ever so sweetly around a purchased angel food cake. Use any sort of Halloween candy or favor you like to complete your presentation.

SERVES 12 TO 16
MAKES ONE 9-INCH CAKE

EQUIPMENT

10-inch cake plate (see page 14), for serving

Small offset spatula

Disposable decorating bag

Assorted eggcups and salt wells, for serving

One purchased 9-inch angel food cake

2 recipes Seven Minute Frosting (page 21), at room temperature

Small sugar candy eyes, 2 for each ghost

1. Place the cake on the cake plate. Reserve 1 cup of frosting to make additional ghost figures. Using an offset spatula, fill the hole in the center of the cake with frosting and then spread frosting over the top and sides in a wavy pattern.

2. Add the reserved frosting to the decorating bag; snip off the tip of the bag to create a ⅛-to ¼-inch opening.

3. Referring to the photo, pipe as many ghosts as you like onto and around the cake and into the eggcups. For each, apply pressure to squeeze out some frosting for a base, then lift the bag slowly, decreasing the pressure until the ghost is the desired size; stop the pressure and lift off the bag. Add 2 candy eyes to each ghost.

27

Purchase sugar candy eyes if you don't wish to draw the icing eyes. A yellow cake mix is a fine alternative for baking quick cupcakes.

CLOWN AROUND CUPCAKES

Let the kids help decorate these funny faces—put the top-pings into small bowls so they can place the decorations after you frost the tops.

MAKES 24 STANDARD CUPCAKES

EQUIPMENT

Pans for 24 standard cupcakes

Paper cupcake liners

Toothpick

Wire cooling racks

Small offset spatula

Coupler and tip for decorating icing

Large serving platter

1 recipe Yellow Cake batter (page 17), or 24 store-bought plain cupcakes

1 recipe Creamy White Frosting (page 21), or one 1-pound can vanilla frosting

12 cups colorful breakfast cereal (such as Trix)

24 small round red candies (such as M&M's or Skittles)

24 gummy worms (such as Brite Crawlers), in assorted colors

One 4.25-ounce tube black decorating icing

1. Preheat the oven to 350 °F. Fit 24 standard cup-cake cups with paper liners. Fill the liners two-thirds full with batter and bake the cupcakes until a tooth-pick inserted into the center comes out clean, 10 to 12 minutes. Cool in cupcake pan for 15 minutes, then turn out onto wire racks to cool completely.

2. Using a small spatula, frost the top of each cupcake.

3. Referring to the photo, arrange about ½ cup breakfast cereal "hair" along the edge of each cup-cake. Press the cereal lightly into the frosting so it adheres.

4. For the noses, press a red candy into the frosting in the center of each cupcake top. For the mouths, press a gummy worm into the frosting, forming a smile shape.

5. Attach a coupler and small round tip to the tube of black icing, and draw an X on the frosting for each eye.

6. Arrange the cupcakes on the platter for serving.

SEA CASTLE

Run with this idea—use a sheet cake base instead of the round one and create a larger grouping of castles. Or make mini-castles (inverted cupcakes will look like bucketfuls of sand) so each child can have one of his or her own.

SERVES 20 TO 26
MAKES ONE 9-BY-10-INCH CAKE

EQUIPMENT

Two 8-inch square cake pans

One 12-inch round cake pan

Waxed or parchment paper

Toothpicks

Wire cooling racks

Cutting board

Long serrated knife

Small offset spatula

Large cake stand or 14-inch cardboard base (see page 14), for serving

Small spoon

Three 4-inch-square colorful foil sheet candy wrappers or foil wrapping paper, for pennants

Scotch tape

2 tablespoons shortening

2 tablespoons flour

2 recipes Marble Cake batter (page 18)

2 recipes Creamy White Frosting (page 21), 1 tinted pale brown, 1 tinted light blue

½ cup light brown sugar, for beach sand

3 sugar ice cream cones

About 25 caramel candy cubes, unwrapped

About 25 Tootsie Roll Midgies candies, unwrapped

¼ cup blue nonpareil sprinkles (or more if needed)

¼ to ½ cup candy rocks

1. Preheat the oven to 350 °F. Lightly grease the bottom of each cake pan, then line it with waxed paper or parchment paper and grease and lightly flour the bottom and sides. Fill the prepared pans two-thirds full with batter and bake the cakes until a toothpick inserted into the center comes out clean, 30 to 35 minutes. Cool the cakes completely in the pans on cooling racks and then turn them out onto the racks.

2. One at a time, place the cooled square cakes on a cutting board and, using the serrated knife, cut each vertically into four 4-inch squares. Using an offset spatula, spread brown frosting over the top of 3 of the squares; place an unfrosted square on top of each. Spread frosting over the top of 1 of the stacks and place another unfrosted square on top of it. Eat the remaining cake square or discard it.

3. Place the round cake on the cake stand. Using a clean offset spatula, spread blue frosting over the top and sides of this cake. Using a clean spatula, spread brown frosting over the top and sides of each multilayer square cake; carefully transfer each square cake to the top of the blue cake, arranging as shown in the photo.

4. Crumble the brown sugar on top of the blue cake, and around the brown cakes. Invert an ice cream cone on the top of each brown cake. Place 8 caramel candies on top of each brown cake, placing 1 at each corner and 1 in the middle of each edge.

5. Using your fingers or a rolling pin, flatten some of the Tootsie Rolls. Create an arched door for each castle using the flattened rolls; also cut out 2 windows for each. Using a dab of frosting to adhere each, place the doors and windows on the castles as shown. Referring to the photo, use your fingers to mold more of the Tootsie Rolls into 12 small balls and 3 larger balls; place them on top of the caramels and ice cream cone tips as shown.

6. Spoon the nonpareil sprinkles onto the cake plate, forming a ring around the base of the round cake. Arrange the candy rocks on top of the nonpareils and also randomly around the castles. Cut a pennant shape from each foil candy wrapper; wrap each around a toothpick, securing with tape. Insert a pennant in the ball on top of each ice cream cone.

You can arrange
this cake directly on a
serving platter, placing the
ribbon end next to it when you
are finished decorating. Cover
the ribbon end with a dab
of frosting and top the dab
with a raspberry.

BERRY CUTE KITE CAKE

Use any fruit you like to create the kite pattern on the cake top—just be sure it's dry so it doesn't bleed color into the frosting. And by all means, instead of triangles, go for stripes or any other kite pattern you fancy.

SERVES 7 TO 10
MAKES ONE 9-BY-13-INCH CAKE

EQUIPMENT

One 9-by-13-inch cake pan

Waxed or parchment paper

Toothpick

Wire cooling racks

Cutting board

Ruler

Long serrated knife

1 cardboard base at least
10 ½ by 13 ½ inches, to cut into a kite shape

Small offset spatula

Decorating bag and #133 star tip

½ yard red 1-inch-wide ribbon, cut in 4 equal pieces with angled ends

4 white wire ties or white string

½ yard red-and-white-striped ½-inch-wide ribbon

Large platter (see page 14), for serving

1. Preheat the oven to 350 °F. Lightly grease the bottom of the cake pan, then line it with waxed paper or parchment paper and grease and lightly flour the bottom and sides. Fill the prepared pan two-thirds full with batter and bake the cake until a toothpick inserted in the center comes out clean, 30 to 35 minutes. If you wish, refer to the chart on page 15 to bake the surplus batter in a smaller pan. Cool the cake completely in the pan on a cooling rack and then turn it out onto the rack.

2. Place the cooled cake on a cutting board. Using a ruler and serrated knife, cut the cake into the pieces shown in the cutting diagram (see page 34).

3. Arrange the cake pieces on the cardboard base as shown in the layout diagram (see page 34). Cut the base to fit the cake.

4. Reserve ¾ cup of frosting for decorating. Using an offset spatula, bond adjacent cake pieces with a thin layer of frosting. Eat the 2-by-5-inch piece that isn't needed or discard it. Frost the top and sides of the cake with the remaining frosting.

5. Referring to the photo, use the edge of a spatula or a skewer to lightly divide the cake top into 4 sections. Set aside 1 large raspberry. Working from the interior out to each point, arrange the fruit in neat rows inside each section as shown; leave a little margin uncovered at the perimeter. →

1 tablespoon shortening

1 tablespoon flour

1 recipe Yellow Cake batter
(page 17)

1 recipe Creamy White Frosting
(page 21)

2 pints (about 4 cups) fresh
blueberries, rinsed, drained, and
completely dried

2 pints (about 4 cups) fresh
raspberries, rinsed, drained, and
completely dried

→ **6.** Fit the decorating bag with the star tip. Transfer the reserved frosting to the bag.

7. Pipe rosettes around the top perimeter of the cake. For each, use even pressure to squeeze out a small dome of frosting, then raise the tip and decrease the pressure to make a point; stop the pressure and reposition the tip for the next rosette.

8. Referring to the photo, tie the red ribbons with wire ties or string in pairs to the striped ribbon. Lay the striped ribbon over 1 corner (or the end) of the platter. Carefully transfer the cake on the base to the platter. Place the reserved raspberry on the ribbon next to the cake.

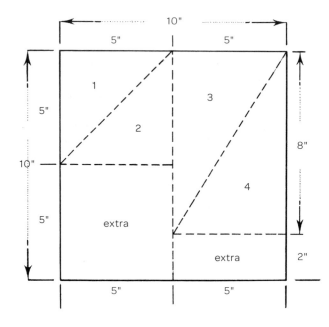

CUTTING DIAGRAM

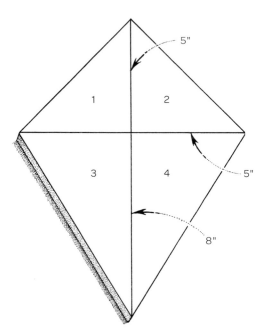

LAYOUT DIAGRAM

CHOCOLATE MOOSE

Make this moose for a school party. Or transform him into a reindeer for winter holidays—just move the antlers toward the top of the head and add a red jawbreaker candy instead of nostrils so he looks like you-know-who.

SERVES 12 TO 14
MAKES ONE 10-BY-12-INCH CAKE

EQUIPMENT

Pans for 27 mini cupcakes

Paper mini cupcake liners

Toothpick

Wire cooling racks

2 small bowls

Small offset spatula

Platter or cardboard base (see page 14), for serving

Decorating bag and #2A round tip

Coupler and round tip, for decorating icing

Very small spoon

1. Preheat the oven to 300 °F. Fit the pans with paper liners. Fill the liners two-thirds full with batter and bake the cupcakes until a toothpick inserted into the center comes out clean, 6 to 8 minutes. If you wish, bake the surplus batter as more mini cupcakes, or refer to the chart on page 15 to bake in a small pan. Cool the cupcakes in the pans on a cooling rack for 15 minutes and then turn out onto the rack to cool completely.

2. While the cupcakes are cooling, divide the frosting equally into 2 small bowls. Tint the frosting in 1 bowl brown (see page 12). Mix the peanut butter into the frosting in the other bowl.

3. Using an offset spatula, spread brown frosting on 17 cupcake tops. Using a clean spatula, spread peanut butter frosting on the 10 remaining cupcake tops. Reserve the remaining peanut butter frosting to add to the antlers later.

4. Referring to the photo, arrange the cupcakes on the serving platter.

5. Fit the decorating bag with the round tip. Transfer the reserved peanut butter frosting to the bag. Pipe the frosting into antlers on top of the peanut butter cupcakes as shown. →

35

When you arrange the cupcakes on the platter, put a little dab of frosting under each to keep it in position.

1 recipe Chocolate Cake batter
(page 16), or one 18.25-ounce
chocolate cake mix

1 recipe Creamy White Frosting
(page 21)

Brown gel or paste food color

¾ cup creamy peanut butter

2 ounces white fondant

One 4.25-ounce tube black
decorating icing

Brown sugar (light or dark),
for sprinkling

→ **6.** Using your fingers, flatten and shape 2 pieces of fondant into ovals for the eyes; the ovals should be about as long as the diameter of a cupcake. Place the ovals on top of the brown cupcakes as shown. To make eyelids, shape 2 small pieces of fondant into tiny strings and curve 1 along the top of each oval.

7. Attach a coupler and a small round tip to the tube of black icing. For pupils, make a dot of icing on each white oval. For nostrils, outline an oval of icing on each of the cupcakes at the tip of the moose's nose. Using a very small spoon, sprinkle a little brown sugar into the lower part of each nostril.

To support the tusks above the platter, insert a toothpick partway into the wide end of each, then insert the other end into the side of the cake. If you have some Royal Icing (page 20) or purchased cookie icing, use it as glue to supplement the bond.

ELLY THE ELEPHANT

They say an elephant never forgets; perhaps this one has a funny story to tell your assembled guests. If you bake the extra batter in a 6-inch round pan, you can make a baby elephant too.

SERVES 6 TO 8
MAKES ONE 10-BY-12-INCH CAKE

EQUIPMENT

One 10-inch round pan

Waxed or parchment paper

Toothpicks

Wire cooling racks

Cutting board

Long serrated knife

Small offset spatula

Medium-mesh sieve

Large platter or 14-inch cardboard base (see page 39), for serving

1 tablespoon shortening

1 tablespoon flour

1 recipe Chocolate Cake batter (page 16)

1 recipe Creamy White Frosting (page 21), tinted pink

2 chocolate chips

2 white wafer candies (such as Necco Wafers)

4 ounces (½ cup) white fondant (such as Wilton Ready-to-Use Rolled Fondant)

1. Preheat the oven to 350 °F. Lightly grease the bottom of the cake pan, then line it with waxed paper or parchment paper and grease and lightly flour the bottom and sides. Fill the prepared pan two-thirds full with batter. Bake the cake until a toothpick inserted in the center comes out clean, 30 to 35 minutes. If you wish, refer to the chart on page 15 to bake the surplus batter in a small pan or in cupcake cups. Cool the cake completely in the pan on a cooling rack and then turn it out onto the rack.

2. Place the cooled cake on a cutting board. Referring to the cutting diagram (see page 40) and using a toothpick, prick the outline of the head and ears into the top of the cake. You can make a paper pattern first if you like. Using the serrated knife, cut the cake along the pricked outlines. Eat the scraps or discard them.

3. Using an offset spatula, spread the frosting over the top and sides of each piece. To add texture to the "skin," lightly press the frosting all over with a kitchen sieve. Arrange the pieces on the platter as shown in the photo. Blend the frosting where the head and ears abut; press the blended areas with the sieve too.

4. Using a dab of frosting, affix each chocolate chip to a white candy wafer, placing the chip near the edge of the wafer as shown. Affix the wafers on the cake for eyes. →

→ **5.** To make each tusk, roll some fondant between your palms, making a cone about 1 inch across at the base and 3 inches long. Referring to the photo, shape the bases at an angle, curve the tusks slightly, and invert them against the elephant's trunk; affix with a dab of frosting.

6. For the eyebrows, roll some more fondant into two 1½-inch-long strings and curve each above an eye. For the ear accents, roll two 3-inch-long, fondant strings and curve one on the inside top edge of each ear. Lightly press the fondant into the frosting.

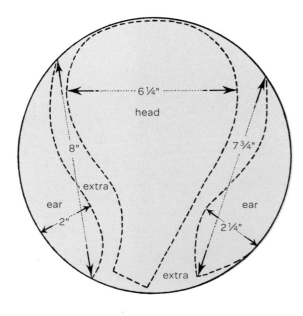

CUTTING DIAGRAM (10" CIRCLE)

GREEN GARDEN GRASSHOPPER

If you wish to assemble the grasshopper on a cardboard base before placing it on the serving platter, make the base exactly the size of the assembled cakes. Transfer the base with the cakes to the platter before adding the legs.

SERVES 10 TO 14
MAKES ONE 6-BY-14-INCH CAKE

EQUIPMENT

One 6-inch round cake pan

One 8-inch round cake pan

Waxed or parchment paper

Toothpick

Wire cooling racks

Cutting board

Long serrated knife

Small offset spatula

Decorating bag and #9 round tip

Platter or 7-by-15-inch cardboard base (see page 14), for serving

Small spoon

Rolling pin

¾-inch round piping tip

Small, sharp knife

2 yellow miniature taper candles (5 inches long)

PLATTER EMBELLISHMENTS

Silk greenery (see photo)

Yellow nonpareil sprinkles

Green jellybeans

Candy daffodil cake decorations

1. Preheat the oven to 350 °F. Lightly grease the bottom of each cake pan, then line it with waxed paper or parchment paper and grease and lightly flour the bottom and sides. Fill the prepared pans two-thirds full with batter. Bake until a toothpick inserted in the center comes out clean, 20 to 25 minutes for the 6-inch pan, and 30 to 35 minutes for the 8-inch pan. If you wish, refer to the chart on page 15 to bake the surplus batter in a small pan or in cupcake cups. Cool the cakes completely in the pans on cooling racks and then turn them out onto the racks.

2. Place the cooled cakes on a cutting board. Do not level their tops. Using a long serrated knife, cut each in half vertically to make half-rounds. Turn one 8-inch half-round over so the flat side is up and, using an offset spatula, spread the leaf green frosting over it. Then, stack the other 8-inch half-round on top of it, rounded side up. Using a clean spatula and the lime green frosting, repeat with the 6-inch half-rounds. Turn each layered cake so the curved edge is up (don't butt them together yet) and spread lime green frosting over the top and both sides of each. Add more frosting to the sides to give the cakes a domed shape, as shown in the photo.

3. Fit the decorating bag with the round tip. Add ½ cup leaf green frosting to the bag. To create wings on the larger cake section, refer to the photo and pipe an outline for the wing tips on top of the lime green frosting. Then, working from the outline to the other end of the cake, cover the wing area with leaf green frosting. Continue to pipe the frosting from the bag, spreading it to cover the lime green frosting with a clean offset spatula as you go. →

When you are frosting a specific area like the grasshopper's wings, it's much easier to control the results if you apply the frosting through a decorating bag—just spreading it on is not a shortcut!

2 tablespoons shortening

2 tablespoons flour

1 recipe Chocolate Cake batter
(page 16)

2 recipes Creamy White Frosting
(page 21), 1 tinted leaf green,
1 tinted lime green

Eight 7-inch pretzel rods

One 10-ounce bottle white
cookie icing

Yellow nonpareil sprinkles, for feet

2 ounces yellow fondant (such as
Wilton Ready-to-Use Rolled Fondant)

2 pieces black coated-licorice candy
(such as Good & Plenty)

1 flat stick striped chewing gum

→ **4.** Arrange the frosted cakes end-to-end on the serving platter as shown. Pipe a line of leaf green frosting all around the base of the assembled cake.

5. To make the back leg on each side of the cake, arrange 2 pretzel rods in an inverted V as shown, pressing them lightly into the frosting on the cake's side. Following the manufacturer's directions, squeeze a small pool of white icing onto the platter around the base of each rod, and place a dab of icing between the rods where they cross at the top. For each front leg, break a pretzel rod in half and arrange on the cake as shown; add a pool of icing around each. Break another rod into 1-inch pieces and place 1 piece for each foot. Using a small spoon filled with a small amount of nonpareils, sprinkle nonpareils over each pool of icing.

6. For the eyes, roll out a small piece of fondant. Using the wide end of a piping tip (¾ inch in diameter), cut out 2 circles. Put a dab of white icing on the back of each circle and place 1 on each side of the head. Use a dab of icing to affix a piece of licorice to each eye.

7. For the tongue, use a small, sharp knife to cut a notch in 1 end of the gum stick; bend the stick and insert it near the base of the face as shown. For the antennae, pipe 2 dots of green frosting onto the top of the head. Insert a candle into each dot.

8. Referring to the photo, arrange the silk greenery on the platter (affix with dabs of frosting). Sprinkle some nonpareils onto the platter. Add the jellybeans and candy daffodils (affix the daffodils with a dab of frosting if you want to keep them upright).

If you are right-handed, work from left to right to arrange the graham crackers (vice versa for lefties) to help prevent smearing the iced crackers as you work.

HAPPY BIRTHDAY TOMMY TEN

WORD PLAY

Crossword fans will adore this puzzle cake. You can whip it up in no time—simply begin with a bakery-made frosted half-sheet cake and use purchased tubes of decorating icing to top the graham cracker letter tiles.

SERVES 16 TO 24
MAKES ONE 12-BY-16-INCH CAKE

EQUIPMENT

One 12-by-16-inch half-sheet cake pan

Waxed or parchment paper

Toothpick

Wire cooling racks

Small offset spatula

Decorating bag and #6 round tip

Large platter or 20-inch cardboard base (see page 14), for serving

Decorating bag and #22 star tip

1 tablespoon shortening

1 tablespoon flour

2 recipes Chocolate Cake batter (page 16), or bakery-made half-sheet cake

64 chocolate-covered graham crackers, each 1¾ by 1¼ inches

2 recipes Creamy White Frosting (page 21), ½ cup tinted red

1. Preheat the oven to 325 °F. Lightly grease the bottom of the cake pan, then line it with waxed paper or parchment paper and grease and lightly flour the bottom and sides. Fill the prepared pan two-thirds full with batter and bake the cake until a toothpick inserted in the center comes out clean, 50 to 60 minutes. Cool the cake completely in the pan on a cooling rack and then turn it out onto the rack.

2. Plan your message while the cake is cooling. On a piece of paper, draw a grid to represent the graham crackers, making it 8 crackers wide and 8 crackers long—don't worry about making it perfect; it's just a sketch. Decide how to arrange your message on it, writing the needed letters on the cracker sketch.

3. Count out the graham crackers and lay them out on a work surface. Using an offset spatula, frost the top of each with white frosting, making it as smooth as you can (dip the spatula in hot water and dry it to help smooth; see page 13). Run a fingertip around the edge of each to clear a chocolate border.

4. Fit a decorating bag with the round tip; add the red frosting to the bag. Pipe the appropriate letter onto each frosted graham cracker.

5. Place the cooled cake on the platter. Spread white frosting over the top and sides. Fit another decorating bag with the star tip; add ¾ cup white frosting to the bag. Pipe stars around the bottom perimeter of the cake. For each star, hold the bag straight up with the tip against the cake; squeeze the bag, keeping the tip in the frosting until the star forms; stop the pressure and reposition the tip for the next star.

6. Arrange the graham crackers on top of the cake in the pattern you sketched.

TOM

MAX

ZOE

Food writers
such as Foodoodlers (see
Resources, page 128) are like
markers with edible ink—
an ingenious invention for
adding detail, like names,
to candy and other
hard surfaces.

HERE, KITTY KITTY

Use whatever color frosting says "kitty" to you—tint ready-made vanilla or the Creamy White Frosting from the recipe on page 21. Start with purchased unfrosted cupcakes so you can focus your time on decorating the kitty faces.

MAKES 24 STANDARD CUPCAKES

EQUIPMENT

Small offset spatula

Small, sharp knife

Large serving platter

24 store-bought unfrosted vanilla cupcakes

One 12-ounce container ready-made chocolate frosting

One 12-ounce container ready-made vanilla frosting, tinted light brown (page 12)

One 14-ounce package cherry-flavor Pull-n-Peel Twizzlers licorice candy

24 flat sticks white chewing gum (such as Doublemint or Juicy Fruit)

6 flat sticks pink chewing gum

1 brown or green food writer

48 sugar candy eyes

24 NECCO Wafers

1. Using a small spatula, frost the top of each cupcake. Use chocolate frosting for half the cupcakes and tinted vanilla frosting for the other half.

2. For the mouths, peel off strips of the licorice candy and cut into 2-inch lengths. Arrange 2 lengths on each cupcake in a rounded W shape.

3. For ears, use a small, sharp knife to cut a triangle from each white stick of gum. Make the triangles about ¾ inch wide at the base and 1½ inches tall in the center. Color in the inner ear using the food writers. Cut the pink sticks of gum into small triangles for the noses. Referring to the photo, insert 2 white triangles into the frosting on each cupcake for the ears; press a pink nose onto each cupcake above the mouth.

4. Use the food writer to color a pointed oval around the black dot in the center of each sugar candy eye. Press 2 eyes into the frosting on top of each cupcake. Cut sticks of white gum into whiskers, about ⅛ by 2 inches each. Insert 3 whiskers at each end of the mouth on each cupcake. Place a dab of frosting on the back of each NECCO Wafer and adhere it to the cupcake paper. If desired, use the food writer to write party guests' names on the wafers.

5. Arrange the cupcakes on the platter for serving.

WORLD CUP SOCCER BALL

Interlocking pentagons are hard to draw freehand, so I was delighted to find a soccer ball mold that has outlines to follow when frosting (see Resources, page 128). Once you have the mold, this cake is simple to create. If there's a soccer fan in your family, you'll find the pan a worthwhile investment.

SERVES 10 TO 14
MAKES ONE 4 ½-BY-9-INCH CAKE

EQUIPMENT

One 4 ½-by-9-inch half-sphere soccer ball cake pan

Toothpick

Wire cooling racks

2 decorating bags and two #9 round tips

10-inch cake plate or cardboard base (see page 14), for serving

Small offset spatula

Tall thin pink taper candles (optional)

1 tablespoon shortening

1 tablespoon flour

1 recipe Yellow Cake batter (page 17)

1 recipe Creamy White Frosting (page 21), ½ tinted bright pink

About 30 round green candies (such as Everlasting Gobstoppers or small jawbreakers)

5 round yellow candies

1. Preheat the oven to 350 °F. Lightly grease the bottom of the cake pan and lightly flour the bottom and sides. Fill the prepared mold two-thirds full with batter. Bake the cake until a toothpick inserted into the center comes out clean, 25 to 30 minutes. If you wish, refer to the chart on page 15 to bake the surplus batter in a small pan or as cupcakes. Cool the cake completely in the pan on a cooling rack and then turn it out onto the rack.

2. Fit each of the decorating bags with a round tip. Add the pink frosting to 1 bag and the white frosting to the other bag.

3. Place the cooled cake on the serving plate. Referring to the photo and following the molded detail on the cake, pipe the outline of the top pentagon with pink frosting. Pipe more frosting inside the outline, spreading with an offset spatula to fill the outline. Working on 1 section at a time, outline and fill in the rest of the pink pentagons. Pipe along the molded ribs between the pink pentagons. In the same way, outline and fill each remaining area with white frosting, spreading with a clean offset spatula.

4. Create a flower design in the center of each full white pentagon as shown in the photo; press the candies gently into the frosting to adhere. If you wish, arrange candles on top when ready to serve.

Tint half of
the frosting black
instead of pink for
a more traditional
soccer ball.

Gumdrop heads attach to cupcake bodies with a toothpick. Remove it before taking a bite!

FLYAWAY LADYBUGS

Mix up the frosting colors on these adorable insects—yellow and orange also look great.

MAKES 24 STANDARD CUPCAKES

EQUIPMENT
Pans for 24 standard cupcakes
Paper cupcake liners
25 toothpicks or 2-inch-long pieces of lollipop stick
Wire cooling racks
Small offset spatula
Small microwave-safe dish
Plastic food-storage bag
Skewer
Large serving platter

1 recipe Chocolate Cake batter (page 16)
1 recipe Creamy White Frosting (page 21), tinted red
1 cup chocolate chips
About 150 brown mini M&M's candies
About 25 large black gumdrops
About 50 coated black licorice pieces (such as Good & Plenty)
One 10-ounce bottle white cookie icing
About 50 sugar candy eyes
Daisy sugar candies, for presentation (optional)

1. Preheat the oven to 350 °F. Fit the cupcake cups with paper liners. Fill them two-thirds full with batter and bake the cupcakes until a toothpick inserted in the center comes out clean, 10 to 12 minutes. Cool the cupcakes in the pans on a cooling rack for 15 minutes and then turn out onto the rack to cool completely.

2. Using an offset spatula, spread red frosting over the top of each cooled cupcake. Dip the spatula in hot water, wipe it dry, and smooth the frosting.

3. Melt the chocolate chips in the microwave. Put them in a microwave-safe dish; microwave for 40 seconds, then stir. Microwave again for 10 or 15 seconds; stir. Repeat until the chocolate is melted and smooth. Transfer the melted chocolate to the plastic food-storage bag; cut off 1 corner of the bag, leaving a small opening.

4. Referring to the photo, pipe the wing outlines onto the top of each cupcake with the chocolate. Press 3 mini M&M's candies onto each wing area as shown.

5. Refer to the photo to decorate the heads: Using a skewer, poke 2 holes in the side of each gum-drop near the base; insert a piece of licorice in each for antennae. Use dabs of cookie icing to adhere the candy eyes in front of the licorice. Insert a toothpick or lollipop stick in the bottom of each gumdrop and then insert it in the side of a cupcake, just below the top.

6. Arrange the ladybugs on the platter. Decorate the platter with daisy candies if you wish.

EASTER EGG CAKE

When you've colored enough Easter eggs, decorate this holiday cake for a sweet diversion. Make a second, smaller egg with the surplus batter and decorate it to complement this one. While one batch of frosting will be enough for both, you'll need additional decorations.

SERVES 6 TO 8
MAKES ONE 8-BY-10-INCH CAKE

EQUIPMENT

One 10-inch round or egg-shaped cake pan

Waxed or parchment paper

Toothpicks

Wire cooling racks

Cutting board

Long serrated knife

Platter or 12-inch cardboard base (see page 14), for serving

Small offset spatula

Decorating bag and #6 round tip

1 tablespoon shortening

1 tablespoon flour

1 recipe Yellow Cake batter (page 17)

1 recipe Creamy White Frosting (page 21), 2½ cups tinted light blue, ½ cup tinted yellow

About 10 one-inch daisy sugar candies

About 40 half-inch pink drop flower candies

About 20 three-quarter-inch daisy sugar candies

1. Preheat the oven to 350 °F. Lightly grease the bottom of the cake pan, then line it with waxed paper or parchment paper and grease and lightly flour the bottom and sides. Fill the prepared pan two-thirds full with batter. Bake the cake until a toothpick inserted in the center comes out clean, 30 to 35 minutes. If you wish, refer to the chart on page 15 to bake the surplus batter in a small pan or as cupcakes. Cool the cake completely in the pan on a cooling rack and then turn it out onto the rack.

2. Place the cooled cake on a cutting board. If you have a round cake, refer to the photo and use a toothpick to prick the outline of the egg shape into the top. You can make a paper pattern first if you like (see page 10). Using the serrated knife, cut out the egg along the pricked outline; eat the scraps or discard them. The egg should be 7½ inches wide across the middle and 10 inches long.

3. Transfer the cake to the platter. Using an offset spatula, spread the blue frosting over the top and sides of the cake.

4. Arrange the 1-inch daisy candies in a curved row across the middle of the cake top; lightly press them into the frosting. Add a row of pink drop flowers above and below the daisies.

5. Fit the decorating bag with the round tip; add the yellow frosting to the bag. Pipe a line of frosting above and below the decorations on the cake. Referring to the photo, add the ¾-inch daisies and the remaining pink flowers to the cake. Pipe a line of beads around the top perimeter of the cake. For each bead, use even pressure to squeeze out a small amount of frosting, then release the pressure and lift the tip.

53

ROYAL CROWN

What better way to make your little king or queen feel special than with a delectable crown? To make everyone at the party royal, provide a festive party crown at each table setting.

SERVES 9 TO 12
MAKES ONE 9-BY-11-INCH CAKE

EQUIPMENT

One 9-by-13-inch cake pan

Waxed or parchment paper

Toothpicks

Wire cooling racks

Cutting board

Long serrated knife

Platter or 10-by-12-inch cardboard base (see page 14), for serving

Small offset spatula

Rolling pin

Small, sharp knife

¾-inch round piping tip

Sealable plastic bag

Hammer

Small spoon

1. Preheat the oven to 350 °F. Lightly grease the bottom of the cake pan, then line it with waxed paper or parchment paper and grease and lightly flour the bottom and sides. Fill the prepared pan two-thirds full with batter. Bake the cake until a toothpick inserted in the center comes out clean, 35 to 40 minutes. If you wish, refer to the chart on page 15 to bake the surplus batter in a small pan or in cupcake cups. Cool the cake completely in the pan on a cooling rack and then turn it out onto the rack.

2. While the cake is cooling, refer to the pattern in the layout diagram (see page 57) to draw and then cut out a paper pattern for the crown (see page 57). Place the cooled cake on a cutting board. Center the pattern on top of the cake as shown in the layout diagram. Use a toothpick to prick the outline of the crown onto the cake top. Using the serrated knife, cut the cake into the outlined shape. Eat the scraps or discard them.

3. Place the cake on the serving platter. Using an offset spatula, spread frosting over the top and sides of the cake.

4. Using a rolling pin, roll the pink fondant out to 2 by 13 inches. Using a small, sharp knife, cut out one ½-by-13-inch strip and one 1½-by-13-inch strip. Referring to the photo, cut the ends of the strips to follow the shape of the crown sides, and then place the narrower strip on the cake top, parallel to and just above the bottom edge. Place the wider strip on the cake top, parallel to and a short distance above the first strip. →

The candy makes the crown: Sweetly Sour Belts, rock candy, and foil-wrapped chocolate stars make this super-special.

1 tablespoon shortening

1 tablespoon flour

1 recipe Yellow Cake batter
(page 17)

1 recipe Creamy White Frosting
(page 21), tinted yellow

4 ounces (½ cup) pink fondant
(such as Wilton Ready-to-Use Rolled
Fondant)

2 ounces (¼ cup) yellow fondant

One 2-ounce package Airhead
Xtremes Sweetly Sour Belts candy

1 yellow rock candy stick

1 pink rock candy stick

1 purple rock candy stick

Yellow food glitter, for dusting

One 4.25-ounce tube yellow
decorating icing

5 gold foil–wrapped chocolate
star candies

→ **5.** Roll out the yellow fondant to 2 by 10 inches. Cut out 8 diamonds, each about 1¼ inches high and 1 inch wide. Referring to the photo, place the diamonds on the wider pink strip.

6. Cut the Sweetly Sour Belts into strips to decorate the crown points. Make 1 strip 3½ inches long, 2 strips 2½ inches long, and 2 strips 1½ inches long; cut both ends of each strip into points. Place the strips on top of the cake as shown, centering the longest on the center point, the shortest on the outside points, and the remaining 2 strips on the remaining points.

7. Cut 8 small diamonds from the Sweetly Sour Belts, making each smaller than the yellow fondant diamonds. Center 1 on top of each yellow diamond. Using the wide end of a piping tip (¾ inch in diameter), cut 6 circles from the same candy. Place these at even intervals on top of the narrower pink fondant strip on the cake.

8. To break the rock candy into chunks, place all the sticks in the sealable plastic bag. Place on a work surface and tap with a hammer or rolling pin. Arrange the yellow chunks along the top and bottom edges of the wider pink fondant strip. Arrange the pink chunks between the yellow fondant diamonds. Arrange the purple chunks between the striped circles.

9. With the small spoon, sprinkle the top of the cake with the yellow food glitter. Using the tube of decorating icing, outline the bottom perimeter of the cake on the platter.

10. To support the foil-wrapped stars, slide 3 toothpicks into each point of the crown. Place 1 right at the point and 1 on each side of the point, inserting them a little below the top edge of the cake and leaving about 1 inch extending beyond the point. One at a time, place a dab of frosting on the back of each foil-wrapped star and adhere it to the toothpicks as shown. Make sure to remove the toothpicks before eating.

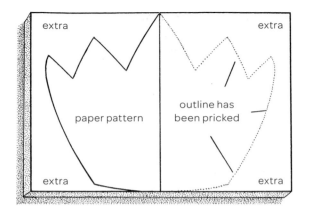

LAYOUT DIAGRAM (CAKE IS 9 BY 13 INCHES)

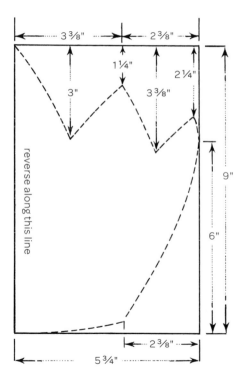

CUTTING DIAGRAM

You can buy single-color M&M's at bulk candy stores. To save time, use ready-made frosting—buy 2 containers.

OVER THE RAINBOW

For a pot of gold that offers each guest a sweet little favor, fill a small bowl with foil-covered chocolate coins and place it at one end of the cake.

SERVES 18 TO 24
MAKES ONE 4-BY-9-BY-4 ½-INCH CAKE

EQUIPMENT

Two 9-inch round cake pans

Waxed or parchment paper

Toothpick

Wire cooling racks

Cutting board

Long serrated knife

Ruler

Small offset spatula

Platter or 8-by-10-inch cardboard base (see page 14), for serving

Long tweezers

2 tablespoons shortening

2 tablespoons flour

1 recipe Chocolate Cake batter (page 16)

2 recipes Creamy White Frosting (page 21)

1 ½ cups each purple, blue, green, yellow, orange, and red M&M's candies

1. Preheat the oven to 350 °F. Lightly grease the bottom of each cake pan, then line it with waxed paper or parchment paper and grease and lightly flour the bottom and sides. Fill the prepared pans two-thirds full with the batter. Bake the cakes until a toothpick inserted in the center comes out clean, 30 to 35 minutes. Cool the cakes completely in the pans on cooling racks and then turn them out onto the racks.

2. One at a time, place each cooled cake on a cutting board and, using a long serrated knife and a ruler as a guide, cut it in half vertically to make two half-moon shapes.

3. Using an offset spatula, spread frosting on the broad surface of one half-round cake. Stack another half-round cake on top. Repeat. You may repeat again with the fourth half-round cake if you like, but 3 layers is probably as thick as you'll want your rainbow to be. Eat the leftover half-round or discard it.

4. Transfer the stacked layers to the serving platter, placing the curved face of the cake up. Spread frosting over the top and both flat faces of the cake.

5. Referring to the photo, arrange the M&M's in a rainbow pattern on the cake. Use long tweezers or your fingers. Beginning and ending at the base, place the red arc along the top of 1 side first. Then place the orange, yellow, green, blue, and purple arcs in sequence on that side. Repeat this process on the opposite side. Decorate the top last, adding the appropriate number of stripes for the thickness of your cake.

59

moderate

When it comes to our children's birthdays, sometimes we want to go the extra mile to create a really special cake—one they'll remember for years. The cakes in this section take some added effort, but they don't require any more skill than most home bakers possess. If you haven't used fondant I encourage you to try it because it opens up a whole world of decorating possibilities, as you'll see with many of the cakes here. Fondant is very easy to work with and is becoming increasingly easier to find in supermarkets and craft stores (see the Resource section, page 128). It gives cakes like Professor Penguin (page 92) and the Let It Rain Umbrella Cake (page 69) a smooth, finished look that usually adds to the wow factor when you serve it.

Whichever cake you create, don't be afraid to stray from my decorating suggestions to make it your own. Theo, a five-year-old whose mom and babysitter combined talents to make him the Pirate Treasure Chest (page 78), told them the cake wouldn't be complete without "keys!" So they handed out pretzel sticks fashioned into treasure-chest keys so the kids at his party could open their cake and get to the candy. Have fun with these projects—it's the whole point!

projects

MOVIE POPCORN CAKE

Serve this at a party where watching a movie is part of the plan. The combination of cake and caramel popcorn is a sure hit. If you wish, use red licorice candy laces or fruit leather instead of fondant—arrange them in a ring to form the circle.

1. Preheat the oven to 350 °F. Lightly grease the bottom of each cake pan, then line it with waxed paper or parchment paper and grease and lightly flour the bottom and sides. Fill the prepared pans two-thirds full with batter. Bake the round cake until a toothpick inserted in the center comes out clean, 30 to 35 minutes, and the rectangular cake until a toothpick inserted in the center comes out clean, 35 to 40 minutes. If you wish, refer to the chart on page 15 to bake any surplus batter in a small pan or cupcake cups. Cool the cakes completely in the pans on cooling racks and then turn them out onto the racks.

2. Shape the popcorn cup: Place the cooled rectangular cake on a cutting board. On one 9-inch end of the cake, measure in 2½ inches from each side and mark by pricking with a toothpick. On the opposite end, measure in ½ inch from each side and prick to mark. Using the serrated knife and the ruler as a guide, remove a long wedge from each side of the cake by cutting from the mark on one end to the mark on the opposite end. Eat the wedges or discard them. Transfer the cake to the platter, placing the narrower end near the bottom edge of the platter, and providing ample room at the top of the platter for the addition of caramel corn.

3. Cut the round cake in half vertically to make half-rounds. Place one half on the platter, placing the straight edge adjacent to the wider end of the first cake. Using an offset spatula, bond the adjacent cake edges with a thin layer of frosting and then spread frosting over the top of the half-round cake. Place the second half-round cake on top of the first, aligning the edges. →

SERVES 24 TO 28
MAKES ONE 10-BY-17-INCH CAKE

EQUIPMENT

One 8-inch round cake pan

One 9-by-13-inch baking pan

Waxed or parchment paper

Toothpicks

Wire cooling racks

Cutting board

18-inch ruler

Long serrated knife

Large platter or 10-by-14-inch cardboard base (see page 14), for serving

Small offset spatula

Rolling pin

Small, sharp knife

4-inch round cookie cutter or lid

2 tablespoons shortening

2 tablespoons flour

2 recipes Yellow Cake batter
(page 17)

2 recipes Creamy White Frosting
(page 21)

4 ounces (½ cup) red fondant
(such as Wilton Ready-to-Use
Rolled Fondant)

4 ounces (½ cup) white fondant

One 4.25-ounce tube red
decorating icing

12 ounces caramel corn

→ **4.** Spread the remaining frosting over the top and sides of the cake.

5. Using a rolling pin, roll the red fondant into a thin layer 11 by 3 inches. Using a small, sharp knife, cut six 10 ½-by-¼-inch strips from the fondant. Roll the scraps out again and cut a 4-inch-diameter circle (use a cookie cutter or jar lid or make a template and cut with a small, sharp knife).

6. Roll out the white fondant and cut a circle slightly smaller than the red one.

7. Referring to the photo, arrange the red strips lengthwise on the cake; work from the center out and space the strips about ¼ inch apart at the narrow end of the cake and about 1 ¼ inches apart at the wider end. Place the red circle on the cake; center the white circle on top of it. With the tube of icing, write a message or name on the white circle.

8. Using your fingers, press the caramel corn onto the top and sides of the rounded section of the cake.

SUNNY BUTTERFLY

To capture nature's symmetry, make a paper pattern for this cake—when you do, feel free to create a different wing design. Look in a butterfly field guide or ask your child for inspiration.

SERVES 6 TO 8
MAKES ONE 10-BY-10-INCH CAKE

EQUIPMENT

One 9-inch round cake pan

Waxed or parchment paper

Toothpicks

Wire cooling racks

Scissors

Cutting board

Long serrated knife

Small offset spatula

Cake plate or 12-inch round card-board base (see page 14), for serving

Small spoon

Skewer

2 yellow curly birthday candles, for antennae

1 tablespoon shortening

1 tablespoon flour

1 recipe Yellow Cake batter (page 17)

1 recipe Creamy White Frosting (page 21)

One 4.25-ounce tube white decorating icing

Yellow food glitter, for dusting

Bright pink food glitter, for dusting

Orange food glitter, for dusting

One 6-inch pink/white twisted-stripe candy stick

About 20 small yellow candies (such as Necco candy dots)

About 25 small bright pink candies

1. Preheat the oven to 350 °F. Lightly grease the bottom of the cake pan, then line it with waxed paper or parchment paper and grease and lightly flour the bottom and sides. Fill the prepared pan two-thirds full with batter. Bake the cake until a toothpick inserted in the center comes out clean, 30 to 35 minutes. If you wish, refer to the chart on page 15 to bake the surplus batter in another pan or as cupcakes. Cool the cake completely in the pan on a cooling rack and then turn it out onto the rack.

2. While the cake is cooling, make a paper pattern based on the cutting diagram (see page 67). Cut the pattern apart. Arrange the pattern pieces on your table as shown in the layout diagram on page 67. Draw the wing designs on each section as shown in the photo on page 66.

3. Place the cooled cake on a cutting board. Lay the pattern pieces on top as shown in the cutting diagram and use a toothpick to prick the outline of each section onto the cake top. Using the serrated knife, cut the cake into 4 pieces along the pricked outlines.

4. Using an offset spatula, spread the frosting over the top and sides of each cake piece. One at a time, place the paper patterns on top of the cake sections; use a toothpick to pierce the wing designs into the frosting. Using the decorating icing, pipe the outline of each pricked design. →

Curly birthday candles double as antennae for this beautiful birthday cake.

→ **5.** Arrange the cake pieces on the plate as shown in the layout diagram; leave a little space between them. Refer to the photo to see which color to make each part of the wing design. Using a small spoon filled with a small amount of the appropriate food glitter color, sprinkle glitter inside each outline. Use the tip of a skewer to push the glitter into the pointed end of the designs.

6. Lay the candy stick on the center of the butterfly as shown. Arrange the candy dots on the wings. Add the curly candles as antennae.

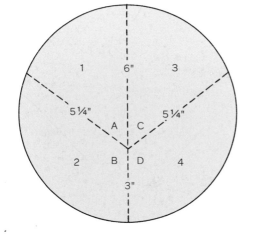

CUTTING DIAGRAM (9" CIRCLE)

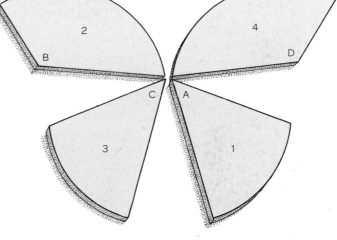

LAYOUT DIAGRAM

When you arrange the cupcakes on the platter, put a little dab of frosting under each to keep it in position.

LET IT RAIN UMBRELLA CAKE

You are invited to use your child's favorite colors for this cake. It's a fun design for a shower too—go with baby colors to welcome a newborn or silver and white for a wedding. The raindrops are optional.

SERVES 12 TO 16
MAKES ONE 13-BY-22-INCH CAKE

EQUIPMENT

Two flat-bottomed 9-inch heart-shaped cake pans

Waxed or parchment paper

Pans for 9 mini cupcakes

9 mini cupcake paper liners

Toothpicks

Wire cooling racks

Scissors

Ruler

2 glass measuring cups

Cutting board

Long serrated knife

Platter or 13-by- 22-inch cardboard base (see page 14), for serving

Small offset spatula

Small spoon

Skewer

Small, sharp knife

Decorating bag and #12 round tip

Small food-safe paintbrush

RAINDROPS

Royal Icing (page 20)

Classic Icing Glaze (page 20)

Blue decorating sugar

2 tablespoons shortening

2 tablespoons flour

2 recipes Yellow Cake batter (page 17)

1 recipe Creamy White Frosting (page 21)

Brown gel or paste food color

Red gel or paste food color

One 4.25-ounce tube purple decorating icing

¼ cup purple decorating sugar

2 tablespoons red decorating sugar

2 tablespoons orange decorating sugar

About 30 small orange candies (such as M&M's)

About 15 small purple candies

About 15 small red candies

4 ounces (½ cup) orange fondant (such as Wilton Ready-to-Use Rolled Fondant)

4 ounces (½ cup) red fondant →

69

1. Preheat the oven to 350 °F. Lightly grease the bottom of each cake pan, then line it with waxed paper or parchment paper and grease and lightly flour the bottom and sides. Fit the mini cupcake cups with paper liners. Fill the prepared pans two-thirds full with batter. Bake the cakes until a toothpick inserted in the center comes out clean, 30 to 35 minutes for the heart-shaped cakes, and 6 to 8 minutes for the cupcakes. If you wish, bake the surplus batter as more cupcakes, or refer to the chart on page 15 to bake in a small pan. Cool the large cakes completely in the pans on cooling racks and then turn them out onto the racks. Cool the cupcakes in the pans on a cooling rack for 15 minutes and then turn out onto the rack to cool completely.

2. While the cakes are cooling, refer to the cutting diagrams on the facing page to make a paper pattern for cutting the cake. Draw the outline of the heart pan twice onto a piece of paper. Cut out 1 of the hearts and cut it in half from the point to the notch between the lobes to make pieces 1 and 2. Measure the length of the edge just cut (from A to B). On the second heart pan outline, draw 2 lines this length, 1 on each side of the heart as shown. Cut out the center portion of this drawing to make piece 3.

3. Transfer ⅔ cup white frosting to a glass measuring cup. Tint it brown (see page 12). Transfer another ⅓ cup white frosting to another glass measuring cup. Tint it red.

4. Place the cooled heart cakes on a cutting board. Using the serrated knife, cut one in half vertically to make pieces 1 and 2. Using the pattern as a guide, prick the outline of piece 3 into the top of the other cake with a toothpick. Cut the cake along the pricked outline. Eat the scraps or discard them.

5. Referring to the layout diagram on the facing page, transfer piece 3 to the platter, orienting it so the point is away from you and close to the end of the platter. Transfer the halved cake to the platter, placing one half on each side of piece 3 to form the umbrella shape. Using an offset spatula, bond the adjacent pieces with a thin layer of white frosting.

6. Spread white frosting over the top and sides of the assembled cake. Using the tube of decorating icing, divide the top of the cake into 8 sections and outline the perimeter as shown in the photo.

7. Referring to the photo and using a small spoon filled with a small amount of purple sugar, slowly sprinkle sugar over 4 sections of the umbrella. Use the tip of a skewer to gently spread the sugar into the narrow area at the top of each section. In the same way, sprinkle red sugar over 2 of the remaining sections and orange sugar over the other 2 sections.

8. Arrange the small orange candies on top of the purple sections of the umbrella, the small purple candies on top of the red sections, and the red candies on top of the orange sections as shown.

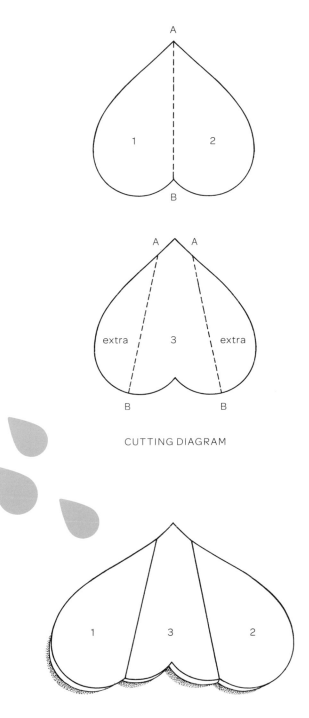

A

1   2

B

A A

extra   3   extra

B   B

CUTTING DIAGRAM

1   3   2

LAYOUT DIAGRAM

9. Spread brown frosting on 5 cupcakes; spread red frosting on the remaining 4 cupcakes. Arrange the cupcakes on the platter to form the umbrella handle.

10. For the umbrella point, roll out each color of fondant into a log shape pointed at one end and thicker at the bottom. With a small knife, cut each point into 3 pieces. Assemble the pieces into 1 multicolored point, using your fingers to mold the fondants into a short striped spire. Insert 1 end of a toothpick into the bottom of the spire; insert the other end of the toothpick into the side of the cake at the top of the umbrella.

11. To make the raindrops, fit a decorating bag with a #12 round tip. Add some Royal Icing to the bag. Spread some waxed paper on your work surface and pipe the raindrops onto it. For each, squeeze some icing from the bag until the base of the drop is the desired size, then decrease the pressure and pull the bag forward to make a point; stop the pressure and lift the bag. Make the drops in assorted sizes. Let them dry until firm.

12. To decorate the raindrops, use a small paintbrush to paint each with Classic Glaze; sprinkle blue sugar on top. Working with 1 drop at a time, lift each off the waxed paper with a small spatula, dab a little icing or frosting on the back, and then arrange it on the serving platter around the cake.

Fashion pom-poms out of coconut-covered donut holes and tie them up with licorice laces.

ICE SKATER'S SPECIAL

If hockey holds sway over figure skating in your house, tint the frosting in the colors of your favorite team and write the team name on the skate.

SERVES 9 TO 12
MAKES ONE 10-BY-14-INCH CAKE

EQUIPMENT

One 10-inch square cake pan

Waxed or parchment paper

Toothpicks

Wire cooling racks

Cutting board

Long serrated knife

Large platter or 11-by-15-inch card-board base (see page 14), for serving

Small offset spatula

Decorating bag and #6 round tip

Skewer

1 tablespoon shortening

1 tablespoon flour

1 recipe Chocolate Cake batter (page 16)

1 recipe Creamy White Frosting (page 21), 2¼ cups tinted red

½ cup shredded sweetened coconut

About 10 white Life Savers candies

2 large candy canes (with crooked ends)

About 5 pieces red string licorice (such as Pull-n-Peel Twizzlers)

2 donut holes, coconut-covered or plain

About 15 white wafer candies (such as Necco Wafers)

1. Preheat the oven to 350 °F. Lightly grease the bottom of the cake pan, then line it with waxed paper or parchment paper and grease and lightly flour the bottom and sides. Fill the prepared pan two-thirds full with batter. Bake the cake until a toothpick inserted in the center comes out clean, 30 to 35 minutes. If you wish, refer to the chart on page 15 to bake the surplus batter in a small pan or as cup-cakes. Cool the cake completely in the pan on a cooling rack and then turn it out onto the rack.

2. Place the cooled cake on a cutting board. Refer-ring to the cutting diagram (see page 74) and using a toothpick, prick the outline of the skate into the top of the cake; you can make a paper pattern first if you like. Using the serrated knife, cut the cake along the pricked outline. Eat the scraps or discard them.

3. Transfer the cake to the platter; leave 6 inches at the bottom for the skate blade. Referring to the photo and leaving a 2-inch band at the cuff unfrosted, spread the red frosting over the top and sides of the skate.

4. Using a clean spatula, spread some of the white frosting over the top and sides of the cuff area. Using your fingers, sprinkle the coconut over the cuff. Referring to the photo, press the Life Savers into the red frosting about 1 inch from the edge of the skate.

5. Fit the decorating bag with the round tip; add the remaining white frosting to the bag. Pipe a curved line along the inside of the Life Savers to define the skate tongue. Referring to the photo, pipe laces across the tongue. Pipe small beads around the →

→ bottom perimeter of the skate. For each, use even pressure to squeeze out a small amount of frosting, then release the pressure and lift the tip.

6. To make the blade, break two 1½-inch-long pieces from 1 candy cane. Wrap short pieces of string licorice around the other candy cane as shown, adhering with dabs of red frosting. Arrange the blade below the skate as shown in the photo on page 72.

7. If using plain donut holes, frost and sprinkle coconut over them. Tie a piece of string licorice in a bow; place at the front of the cuff. Using a skewer, poke the ends of a 6-inch-long piece of licorice into the donut holes; arrange on the platter as shown. Add the white wafer candies to the skate as shown, adhering each with a dab of frosting.

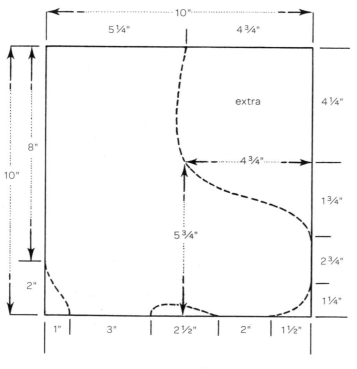

CUTTING DIAGRAM

EXTRA-SWEET PIZZA

You'll have enough batter and frosting here to make two pizzas—just purchase twice the listed amount of marzipan, chocolate, and cinnamon or cocoa to have enough for decorating both.

SERVES 12 TO 16
MAKES TWO 9-INCH CAKES

EQUIPMENT

Two 9-inch round cake pans

Waxed or parchment paper

Toothpicks

Wire cooling racks

Glass measuring cup

Long serrated knife

Small offset spatula

Decorating bag and #1A round tip

Rolling pin

Small, sharp knife

1½-inch round cutter

1¼-inch round cutter

1-inch round cutter

1. Preheat the oven to 350 °F. Lightly grease the bottom of each cake pan, then line it with waxed paper or parchment paper and grease and lightly flour the bottom and sides. Fill the prepared pans two-thirds full with batter and bake the cakes until a toothpick inserted in the center comes out clean, 30 to 35 minutes. Cool the cakes completely in the pan on cooling racks and then turn them out onto the racks. Wash and dry the cake pans for presentation.

2. While the cakes are cooling, transfer 1 cup of the frosting to a glass measuring cup; tint it ivory. Tint the remaining 2 cups of frosting red.

3. Use the serrated knife to level the top of the cooled cakes (see page 10), making them about ½ inch shallower than the pan depth. Return the cakes to the clean pans.

4. Use the spatula to spread the red frosting over the top of the cakes. Fit the decorating bag with the round tip; add the ivory frosting to it. For the crust, pipe along the top perimeter of the cakes, inside the pan.

5. Make the mushrooms: Cut a 4-inch piece from the marzipan roll. Using a rolling pin, roll it to ⅛ inch thick. Using a small knife, cut out 30 mushroom-slice shapes (or use a canapé cutter if you have one). Dip your finger in cinnamon and rub it selectively over the slices to make them look browned. →

You can use cocoa powder instead of ivory food color to tint the frosting for the crust. To join the frosting crust where you begin and end the piping, first dip your finger into cornstarch so it doesn't stick to the frosting, then smooth the join.

2 tablespoons shortening

2 tablespoons flour

1 recipe Yellow Cake batter
(page 17)

1 recipe Creamy White Frosting
(page 21)

Ivory gel or paste food color

Red gel or paste food color

1 pound marzipan

¼ to ½ cup ground cinnamon or
unsweetened cocoa powder

Brown gel or paste food color

Leaf green gel or paste food color

Two 4-ounce white chocolate
bars, grated

→ **6.** Make the pepperoni slices: Cut another 4-inch piece of marzipan. Knead 2 to 3 drops of red food color into it; knead in 1 more drop at a time to give the desired color (add a drop of brown food color if you like). Roll out the marzipan to ⅛ inch thick and use the 1½-inch round cutter to cut out 16 to 20 pieces. Press a paper towel or the bristles of a pastry brush onto each piece to give it some texture. Ripple the edge of each piece slightly with your fingers.

7. Make the pepper rings: Cut another 4-inch piece of marzipan. Knead green food color into it. Roll it between your palms to form a long string. Cut the string into pieces 3 to 3½ inches long and shape each into a lobed ring as shown in the photo.

8. Make the onion rings: Using a rolling pin, roll out the remaining marzipan to ⅛ inch thick. Using the 1¼-inch round cutter, cut out 30 to 36 circles. Using the 1-inch cutter, cut the center from each circle; use the centers for another purpose. Alternatively, cut some or all of the first circles with the 1-inch cutter and remove their centers with the wide end of a piping tip.

9. Arrange the toppings on the pizzas so they look scattered. Sprinkle them with the grated chocolate. When the frosting crust is firm, make it look browned by rubbing it gently with your finger dipped in cinnamon. To serve, cut the cakes into wedges— just like a pizza.

PIRATE TREASURE CHEST

Purchase extra treasure to arrange around the trunk so everyone gets a share of the booty. Or frost the trunk in a pretty color to turn it into a little girl's jewelry box and fill it with candy necklaces.

SERVES 12 TO 16
MAKES ONE 5-BY-9-BY-6-INCH CAKE

EQUIPMENT

One 9-by-13-inch cake pan

Waxed or parchment paper

Toothpick

Wire cooling racks

Glass measuring cup

Cutting board

Ruler

Long serrated knife

Platter or 10-by-10-inch cardboard base (see page 14), for serving

Small offset spatula

Decorating bag and #47 basket weave tip

1. Preheat the oven to 350 °F. Lightly grease the bottom of the cake pan, then line it with waxed paper or parchment paper and grease and lightly flour the bottom and sides. Fill the prepared pan two-thirds full with batter. Bake the cake until a toothpick inserted in the center comes out clean, 35 to 40 minutes. Cool the cake completely in the pan on a cooling rack and then turn it out onto the rack.

2. While the cake is cooling, transfer ½ cup of the frosting to a glass measuring cup; tint it yellow (see page 12). Tint the remainder of the frosting brown.

3. Place the cooled cake on a cutting board. Referring to the cutting diagram (see page 81) and using a ruler and a long serrated knife, cut across the cake 5 inches in from each 9-inch end, leaving a 3-by-9-inch piece in the middle. Cut ½ inch off each end of the middle piece. Referring to step 1 of the assembly diagram (see page 81), cut the middle piece diagonally to make two 8-inch-long wedges. Level the top of one of the 5-by-9-inch pieces, but leave the other one curved to help shape the domed top of the chest.

4. Transfer the piece for the bottom of the trunk to the platter. Center one of the wedges on top of it, aligning the tapered edge with the back 9-inch edge; eat the other wedge or discard it. Using an offset spatula, bond the wedge to the bottom with a thin layer of brown frosting. Spread more brown frosting on top of the wedge and then center the trunk top on the assembled pieces, aligning the back edges as shown in step 2 of the assembly diagram. →

You can make the lock from yellow frosting and some black decorating icing instead of using food clay.

1 tablespoon shortening

1 tablespoon flour

1 recipe Chocolate Cake batter (page 16)

1 recipe Creamy White Frosting (page 21)

Yellow gel or paste food color

Brown gel or paste food color

About 20 small round yellow candies (such as Skittles)

2 ounces (¼ cup) yellow fondant (such as Wilton Ready-to-Use Rolled Fondant)

2 ounces (¼ cup) black fondant

Assorted Ring Pop lollipops

Assorted gold foil-covered chocolate coins

About 5 foil-wrapped miniature chocolate bars

About 5 strings clear rock candy

→ **5.** Using long uneven strokes with the offset spatula to make it look like rustic wood, spread brown frosting over the entire cake. Add extra frosting to the top to emphasize the dome.

6. Fit the decorating bag with the basket weave tip; add the yellow frosting to the bag. For straps, pipe a stripe inset from each end as shown in the photo on page 79; begin at the bottom back and continue up over the top and onto the bottom front. Pipe a handle shape on each bottom end of the trunk. Press the yellow candies onto the straps and also onto each end of each handle as shown.

7. Using your fingers, flatten a piece of yellow fondant and shape it into a ½-inch square for the lock. Shape a piece of black fondant into a keyhole shape and press it into the lock. Center the lock on the front of the trunk top and press it onto the frosting.

8. Break the Ring Pops off their bases (don't worry if the candy breaks; you just want it to look like jewels). Arrange all the candies in and around the open trunk as shown.

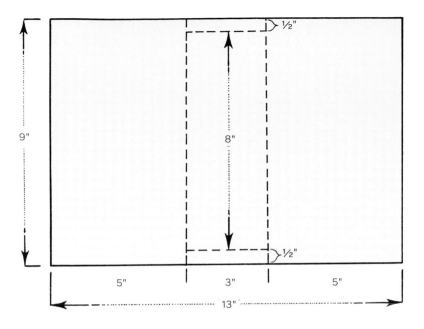

CUTTING DIAGRAM

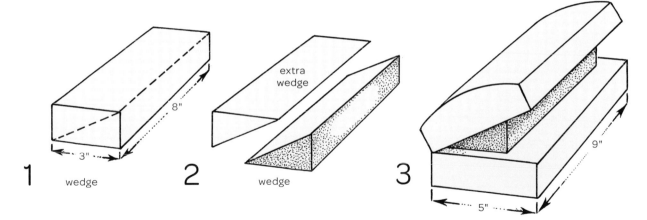

1 wedge

2 extra wedge / wedge

3

ASSEMBLY DIAGRAM

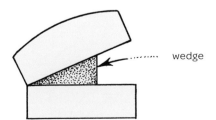

side view

wedge

This cake and surrounding cupcakes will serve a big crowd.

FLORADORABLE

I used Chiclets for the yellow and orange rings around the center of the flower—you may use any small candies you like. To add more color, use tiny red candies instead of piping beads of purple frosting around the perimeter.

SERVES 14 TO 18
MAKES ONE 16-INCH CAKE

EQUIPMENT

One 10-inch round cake pan

Waxed or parchment paper

Pan for 12 standard cupcakes

Paper cupcake liners

Toothpicks

Wire cooling racks

Small offset spatula

Rolling pin

#1A (¾ inch) round piping tip

Decorating bag and #4 round tip

Large platter or 18-inch round cardboard base (see page 14), for serving

1. Preheat the oven to 350 °F. Lightly grease the bottom of the cake pan, then line it with waxed paper or parchment paper and grease and lightly flour the bottom and sides. Fit the cupcake cups with paper liners. Fill the prepared pans and paper liners two-thirds full with batter. Bake until a toothpick inserted in the center comes out clean, 30 to 35 minutes for the 10-inch cake, and 10 to 12 minutes for the cupcakes. There will be quite a bit of extra batter; bake it as more cupcakes or refer to the chart on page 15 to bake in a small pan. Cool the cake completely in the pan on a cooling rack and then turn it out onto the rack. Cool the cupcakes in the pan on a cooling rack for 15 minutes and then turn out onto the rack to cool completely.

2. Using an offset spatula, frost the top and sides of the cooled cake and the top of each cooled cupcake. Reserve the remaining frosting to apply to the cakes later.

3. On a work surface, use a rolling pin to roll the orange fondant out to ⅛ inch thick. Use the wide end of a #1A (¾ inch) piping tip to cut out 30 circles. One at a time, fold each circle almost in half and pinch the layers together at 1 end to form a petal. Set the petals aside to harden. Repeat with the pink fondant.

4. In the same way as in step 3, roll out the green fondant and cut out 26 circles. Don't fold them. Center 1 circle on the top of each cupcake. Referring to the photo, arrange the remaining circles in the center on the top of the large cake. →

83

1 tablespoon shortening

1 tablespoon flour

2 recipes Yellow Cake batter
(page 17)

2 recipes Creamy White Frosting
(page 21), tinted purple

8 ounces (1 cup) orange fondant
(such as Wilton Ready-to-Use
Rolled Fondant)

8 ounces (1 cup) pink fondant

8 ounces (1 cup) green fondant

About 40 pieces yellow Chiclets gum

About 40 pieces orange Chiclets gum

One 4.25-ounce tube white
decorating icing

→ **5.** Referring to the photo, arrange the yellow and orange Chiclets in concentric rings around the group of yellow circles on the top of the large cake.

6. Referring to the photo, arrange 5 fondant petals on top of each cupcake. Place orange petals on 6 cupcakes and pink petals on the other 6 cupcakes.

7. Fit the decorating bag with the #4 round tip. Transfer the remaining frosting to the bag. Pipe small beads around the top perimeter of the large cake. For each, use even pressure to squeeze out a small amount of frosting, then stop the pressure and lift the tip. Pipe a ring of beads inside the ring of yellow Chiclets. Pipe beads along the top edge of each cupcake where there are no petals.

8. Use the tube of decorating icing to add tiny white dots all over the center yellow circle on the top of the large cake. At the base of the petals on top of each cupcake, add an arc of tiny dots to the edge of the yellow circle.

9. Place the large cake in the center of the platter. Arrange the cupcakes around it as shown, placing the beaded edge of each against the cake.

JACK-O'-LANTERN

Bake this for a Halloween party and your guests will be trick-or-treating at your house for years to come.

SERVES 12 TO 16
MAKES ONE 6-BY-7-INCH CAKE

EQUIPMENT

Two 6-inch half-sphere cake pans (such as Wilton Sports Ball set, see Resources, page 128) or two 1½-quart ovenproof bowls

Waxed or parchment paper

Toothpicks

Wire cooling racks

Glass measuring cup

Small offset spatula

Cake plate or 4-inch round cardboard base (optional)

Plastic straw

2 decorating bags, #70 leaf tip, and #5 round tip

Rolling pin

Small, sharp knife

Small plate

Spoon

Compote or shallow bowl, for serving

1. Preheat the oven to 350 °F. Lightly grease the bottom of each cake pan, then line it with waxed paper or parchment paper and lightly grease and flour the bottom and sides. Divide the batter between the pans and bake the cakes until a toothpick inserted in the center comes out clean, 30 minutes. Cool the cakes completely in the pans on cooling racks and then turn them out onto the racks.

2. While the cakes are cooling, transfer ¾ cup of the frosting to a glass measuring cup. Tint it green (see page 12). Tint the remaining frosting orange.

3. Using an offset spatula, spread a thin layer of the orange frosting over the flat surface of 1 cake. Invert the second cake on top of the first, joining the flat surfaces of both domes together. Transfer the assembled cake to the cardboard base, if using, or a cake plate. Cover the cake completely with the rest of the orange frosting.

4. To make rib indentations as shown in the photo on page 86, hold a plastic straw against the cake, curving it from bottom to top. Lift it off, reposition it, and press again. Repeat all around the cake. (Gently incise the ribs with a skewer if you don't have a straw.)

5. For the stem, invert the ice cream cone and, using a clean spatula, cover it with the green frosting; add more frosting at the top to give the stem a curved tip. Place the stem on the top of the cake. →

If you wish to serve this cake in a compote or other shallow bowl as we did, be sure to place it on a cardboard base first so you'll be able to set it in the compote without disturbing your work.

Black decorating sugar gives this pumpkin face a spooky sparkle.

2 tablespoons shortening

2 tablespoons flour

1 recipe Chocolate Cake batter
(page 16)

1 recipe Creamy White Frosting
(page 21)

Green gel or paste food color

Orange gel or paste food color

1 small waffle ice cream cone

4 ounces (½ cup) black fondant
(such as Wilton Ready-to-Use
Rolled Fondant)

Black decorating sugar, for
sprinkling

→ **6.** Fit a decorating bag with a coupler and the leaf tip; add 1 cup of the green frosting to the bag (see page 13). Referring to the photo, pipe several leaves around the base of the stem. Hold the bag at an angle next to the stem. Squeeze out some frosting, allowing it to fan into a wide base, then decrease the pressure and slowly pull the tip away, lifting slightly, to form a point.

7. Remove the leaf tip and replace with the round tip. Pipe tendrils around the stem and leaves. Place the tip where you want the tendril to begin. Using even pressure, squeeze out some frosting and move the tip to draw the tendril. Release the pressure and lift the tip when the tendril is the desired length.

8. Using a rolling pin, roll the fondant to ⅛ inch thick. Referring to the photo and using a small, sharp knife, cut out the features. For the eyes, cut 2 triangles about 1½ inches wide at the base and 1½ inches tall at the center. For the nose, cut another triangle a little smaller than the eyes. Cut the smile to be about 4 inches from tip to tip. You can draw a paper pattern first if you like.

9. Spread the black sugar on a small plate (large enough to hold the smile) using the back of the spoon. Press each cutout into the sugar and then invert the coated cutout onto the pumpkin to form the face, pressing it into the frosting. Transfer the cake to the serving dish if you have not already done so.

SWISHY FISHY

Encourage your kids to help choose colors for the fish. Be sure to have wooden skewers on hand—you'll need them to support the frosted fins.

SERVES 12 TO 16
MAKES ONE 9-BY-13-BY-8-INCH CAKE

EQUIPMENT

Two 8-inch round cake pans

Waxed or parchment paper

Toothpicks

Wire cooling racks

Cutting board

Long serrated knife

Small offset spatula

Platter or 10-by-14-inch cardboard base (see page 14), for serving

Decorating bag and #9 round tip

Wooden skewers

Small spoon

PLATTER EMBELLISHMENTS

Blue decorating icing

Silk greenery

½ cup blue nonpareil sprinkles

Small glass balls (the type used to surround pillar candles)

1. Preheat the oven to 350 °F. Lightly grease the bottom of each cake pan, then line it with waxed paper or parchment paper and grease and lightly flour the bottom and sides. Divide the batter between the pans and bake the cakes until a toothpick inserted in the center comes out clean, 30 to 35 minutes. Cool the cakes completely in the pans on cooling racks and then turn them out onto the racks.

2. Place the cooled cakes on a cutting board. Referring to step 1 of the cutting diagram (see page 90) and using a toothpick, prick the outline of the crescent shape into the top of each cake. The crescent embraces half the circumference of the cake and is 2 inches deep at its middle. You can make a paper pattern first if you like. Using a long serrated knife and carefully separating the sections so you can use the crescents for the fins, cut each cake along the pricked outline. Cut 1 of the crescents in half as shown in step 2 of the cutting diagram; leave the other one whole. Set the whole and halved crescents aside.

3. Make the body: Using an offset spatula, spread some of the light orange frosting over the top of one of the larger pieces of cake. Stack the other piece on top. Transfer the stacked layers to the serving platter, placing the edge from which the crescents were cut down; the weight of the cake will flatten the curve so the fish rests on her belly. Set aside ⅓ cup of the frosting. Spread the remaining light orange frosting over all the surfaces of the cake. Fit the decorating bag with the round tip; add the reserved light orange frosting to it. Pipe a line of frosting around the bottom perimeter of the cake. →

Present this cake on a sea of blue nonpareils studded with silk greenery and small glass balls.

2 tablespoons shortening

2 tablespoons flour

1 recipe Yellow Cake batter
(page 17)

1 recipe Creamy White Frosting
(page 21), 1½ cups tinted light
orange, 1½ cups tinted dark orange

½ cup orange M&M's candies

½ cup yellow M&M's candies

2 white wafer candies (such as
Necco Wafers)

One 4.25-ounce tube black decorating icing

6 ounces (¾ cup) yellow fondant
(such as Wilton Ready-to-Use
Rolled Fondant)

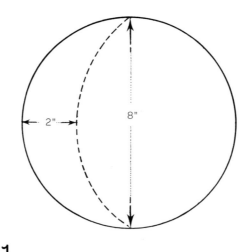

→ **4.** Make the top fin: Using a clean spatula, spread some dark orange frosting over the inside and outside curves of one of the half-crescent pieces. Break two 3-inch-long pieces from a wooden skewer; insert them partway into the bottom of the fin (small flat edge) and then place the fin upright above the body as shown. Secure by inserting the extending skewers into the body. Spread more dark orange frosting over the remaining faces of the fin, being careful not to smear it on the body.

5. Make the side fins: Lay the remaining half-crescent on the cutting board. Holding the knife parallel to the board, slice the half-crescent into 2 equal layers as shown in step 3 of the cutting diagram. Referring to the photo to see how the fins will be positioned, spread some of the dark orange frosting over the inside and outside curved edges, the short flat end, and the top of each; be sure to frost them as a mirrored pair. Lay the fins on the platter next to the body.

6. Make the tail fin: Refer to the photo to see how the fin is positioned against the cake. On the remaining whole crescent, spread more dark orange frosting on the edge that will be the top of the fin; extend the frosting onto the area that will be placed against the back of the body and down to where it will meet

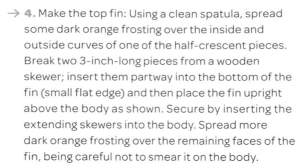

1   CUTTING DIAGRAM (TWO 8" CIRCLES)

the platter. Break two 3-inch-long pieces from a wooden skewer; insert them partway into the middle of the frosted edge of the tail fin; then slide the fin into position against the body, poking the extending skewers into the body as shown in the assembly diagram. Spread the last of the dark orange frosting over the remaining faces of the fin, being careful not to smear it on the body.

7. Decorate the sides and top of the body with the M&M's candies as shown, lightly pressing them into the frosting. Pipe a dot of black decorating icing in the center of each wafer candy; affix each to the fish with a dab of frosting. To make the lips, use your fingers to mold 2 small ovals from the fondant; press them together at 1 end to make a V. With a skewer, poke a small hole into the face end of the body, insert the lips. If they are not secure, remove them, wrap them around a toothpick, and insert the toothpick into the hole.

8. Referring to the photo and using the blue decorating icing, pipe an outline for the ocean onto the platter. Arrange the greenery around the fish (affix with dabs of icing). Spoon nonpareil sprinkles around the fish and greenery, inside the outline. Add the glass balls. When you cut the cake, be sure to separate the fins from the body and remove the skewers.

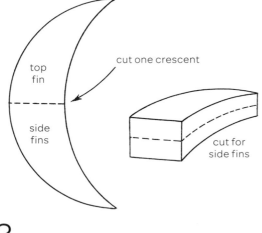

top fin

cut one crescent

side fins

cut for side fins

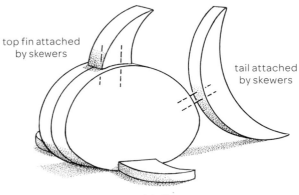

top fin attached by skewers

tail attached by skewers

side fins

2 ASSEMBLY DIAGRAM

3

PROFESSOR PENGUIN

The surface of this smartly attired fellow is textured with finely crushed cookies and shredded coconut. You may omit one or both to suit your taste or speed up the prep time.

SERVES 12 TO 16
MAKES ONE 8½-BY-16-INCH CAKE

EQUIPMENT

One 6-inch round cake pan

One 10-inch round cake pan

Waxed or parchment paper

Toothpicks

Wire cooling racks

Cutting board

Long serrated knife

Large platter or 10-by-17-inch cardboard base (see page 14), for serving

Small offset spatula

Decorating bag and #3 round tip

Small spoon

Small, sharp knife

1. Preheat the oven to 350 °F. Lightly grease the bottom of each cake pan, then line it with waxed paper or parchment paper and grease and lightly flour the bottom and sides. Fill the prepared pans two-thirds full with batter. Bake until a toothpick inserted in the center comes out clean, 20 to 25 minutes for the 6-inch pan, and 30 to 35 minutes for the 10-inch pan. Cool the cakes completely in the pans on cooling racks and then turn them out onto the racks.

2. Place the cooled 10-inch cake on a cutting board. Referring to the photo and using the serrated knife, cut it into an oval for the body: Think of the cake as a clock face and cut from 12:30 to 2; 4 to 5:30; 6:30 to 8; and 10 to 11:30. Eat the scraps or discard them.

3. Transfer the oval to the platter, placing 6 o'clock near the end of the platter. Place the small round cake at the 12 o'clock end of the oval. Using an offset spatula, bond the cakes with a little black frosting where they touch. Then spread black frosting over the sides of the cake.

4. Referring to the photo, use a toothpick to prick the outline of the face into the round cake and the outline of the belly into the oval cake. You can make a paper pattern for each shape first if you wish (see page 10).

5. Fit the decorating bag with the round tip. Fill it with the remaining black frosting. Pipe a line of frosting along the pricked outline made in step 4. Pipe another line along the top perimeter of the joined cakes. →

To keep a neat line between the crumbs and coconut, place a small mound of crumbs near the border and then use the tip of a skewer or the back of a small spoon to spread them out to touch the borders. Work on one area at a time. Do the same thing with the coconut.

2 tablespoons shortening

2 tablespoons flour

1 recipe Chocolate Cake batter (page 16), or one 18.25-ounce chocolate cake mix

2 recipes Creamy White Frosting (page 21), 3 cups tinted black

Classic Icing Glaze (page 20), 1 cup tinted black

1 cup finely crushed chocolate wafer cookies or packaged Oreo Fine Crumbs

1 cup desiccated or very finely shredded sweetened coconut

4 ounces (½ cup) yellow fondant (such as Wilton Ready-to-Use Rolled Fondant)

2 sugar candy eyes

Black licorice lace, for the eyebrows

4 ounces (½ cup) red fondant

1 small red candy (such as M&M's)

→ **6.** Dip a clean offset spatula in warm water and use it to spread the black glaze over the outer portion of the cake top between the piped lines. In the same way, spread the white glaze inside the inner piped outline for the face and belly.

7. Using a small spoon filled with a small amount of crumbs, slowly sprinkle the cookie crumbs onto the black frosting on the top of the cake. In the same way, sprinkle the coconut onto the white frosting.

8. To create the features, use your fingers to mold a small amount of the yellow fondant into 2 narrow triangles for the beak. Pinch them together at the base and insert the beak in the cake as shown. Add the sugar candy eyes. Cut the licorice into small lengths and add them for eyebrows.

9. For the bow tie, use your hands or a small rolling pin to flatten some of the red fondant. Using a small, sharp knife, cut out 2 triangles, making each about 1¾ inches wide at the base and 1¾ inches tall at the center. Arrange them on the cake, placing the small red candy between their tips.

10. For the feet, flatten some more of the yellow fondant to ⅛ inch thick. Cut out 2 triangles, making each about 1¼ inches wide at the base and 1⅜ inches tall at the center. Place them on the cake at the bottom of the belly as shown.

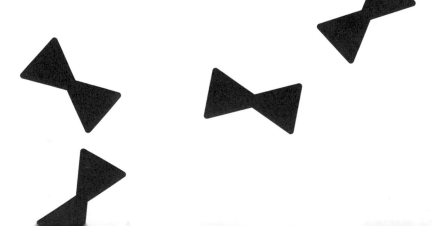

BEACH BALL BLOWOUT

Pool party, anyone? Use a couple of cake mixes to get you started here, and save your effort for the decorating. To give the cake a seaside flavor, scatter a mix of yellow and orange nonpareil sprinkles on the serving plate to simulate sand—purchase extra nonpareil sprinkles if you plan to do this.

SERVES 16 TO 20
MAKES ONE 12-INCH CAKE

EQUIPMENT

Two 12-inch round cake pans

Waxed or parchment paper

Toothpicks

Wire cooling racks

Paper

Scissors

Cake plate or 14-inch round cardboard base (see page 14), for serving

Small offset spatula

Decorating bag and #3 round tip

Small spoon

1. Preheat the oven to 350 °F. Lightly grease the bottom of each cake pan, then line it with waxed paper or parchment paper and grease and lightly flour the bottom and sides. Fill the prepared pans two-thirds full with batter. Bake the cakes until a toothpick inserted in the center comes out clean, 30 to 35 minutes. If you wish, refer to the chart on page 15 to bake the surplus batter in a small pan or cupcake cups. Cool the cakes completely in the pans on cooling racks and then turn them out onto the racks.

2. While the cakes are cooling, refer to the decorating diagram to make a paper pattern for the ball (see page 97).

3. Place 1 cooled cake layer on the cake plate. Set aside ¾ cup of frosting. Using an offset spatula, spread some frosting over the top. Place the second cake layer on top of the first. Frost the sides of the cake.

4. Place the paper pattern on top of the cake. Use a toothpick to pierce the pattern outlines onto the cake top. →

95

Use long tweezers or your fingers to arrange the small candies; tap each lightly to bond it to the glaze.

2 tablespoons shortening

2 tablespoons flour

Two 18.25-ounce chocolate cake mixes

1 recipe Creamy White Frosting (page 21) or one 1-pound can white frosting

1 recipe Classic Icing Glaze (page 20)

One 4-ounce bottle blue nonpareil sprinkles

One 4-ounce bottle orange nonpareil sprinkles

One 4-ounce bottle yellow nonpareil sprinkles

Handful small green candies (such as SweeTarts), for center of ball

→ **5.** Fit the decorating bag with the round tip. Fill it with the reserved frosting. Pipe a line of frosting along the top perimeter of the cake. Pipe along the pattern outlines made in step 4.

6. Dip a clean offset spatula in warm water, wipe it dry, and use it to spread some of the glaze inside each piped section on top of the cake.

7. Referring to the photo and using a small spoon filled with a small amount of nonpareils, slowly sprinkle 1 color of nonpareil over each section. Arrange the small candies in concentric rings inside the round glazed area.

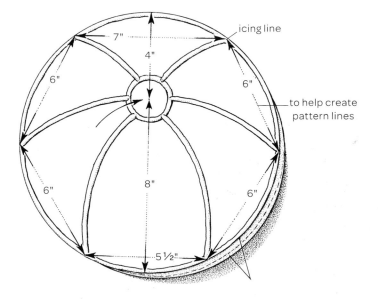

DECORATING DIAGRAM (12" ROUND)

MELT-IN-YOUR-MOUTH SNOWMAN

No need to wait for that perfect snow to create this charming fellow—just break out the mini marshmallows!

SERVES 10 TO 14
MAKES ONE 8-BY-14-INCH CAKE

EQUIPMENT

One 6-inch round cake pan

One 8-inch round cake pan

Waxed or parchment paper

Toothpicks

Wire cooling racks

Large platter or 16-inch cardboard base (see page 14), for serving

Small offset spatula

Rolling pin

Small, sharp knife

Spoon

1. Preheat the oven to 350 °F. Lightly grease the bottom of each cake pan, then line it with waxed paper or parchment paper and grease and lightly flour the bottom and sides. Fill the prepared pans two-thirds full with batter. Bake until a toothpick inserted in the center comes out clean, 20 to 25 minutes for the 6-inch pan, and 30 to 35 minutes for the 8-inch pan. If you wish, refer to the chart on page 15 to bake the surplus batter in cupcake cups. Cool the cakes completely in the pans on cooling racks and then turn them out onto the racks.

2. Referring to the photo, place the cooled cakes next to each other on the platter. Using an offset spatula, bond the cakes with a little frosting where they touch. Then frost the sides of the cakes.

3. Dip a clean offset spatula into warm water, wipe it dry, and use it to spread the glaze over the top of the cakes.

4. Referring to the photo and working from the perimeter toward the center, arrange the mini marshmallows in concentric rings on top of each cake.

5. Place 2 pieces of candy coal on the larger cake for buttons. Arrange some candy coal on the smaller cake for the eyes and mouth as shown. If the candy chunks are too large, place them in a sealable plastic bag on a work surface and lightly tap with a hammer or rolling pin to break them into smaller pieces. →

2 tablespoons shortening

2 tablespoons flour

1 recipe Yellow Cake batter
(page 17)

1 recipe Creamy White Frosting
(page 21)

1 recipe Classic Icing Glaze
(page 20)

6 cups mini marshmallows
(10.5-ounce bag)

Candy coal, black rock candy, or
any black candy, for eyes, mouth,
and buttons

4 ounces (½ cup) orange fondant
(such as Wilton Ready-to-Use
Rolled Fondant)

6 ounces (¾ cup) red fondant

8 ounces (1 cup) white fondant

2 Little Debbie Snow Puff cookies

4 ounces white or clear food glitter

→ **6.** For the nose, mold the orange fondant into a carrot shape about 3½ inches long. Lay it on top of the smaller cake.

7. Using a rolling pin, roll out the red fondant to about ⅛ inch thick. Using a small, sharp knife, cut it into 1-by-1½-inch strips. Roll out the white fondant to the same thickness. Cut it into one 1-by-3½-inch strip and two 1-by-5-inch strips.

8. Referring to the photo, arrange the fondant to be the scarf: Place the red strips at intervals on top of the white strips. Shape 1 end of the shorter white strip so it looks "crushed" and place the strip across the snowman's neck. Cut 1 end of each of the other strips at an angle and layer them on top of the first at 1 side of the neck, placing the pointed ends down.

9. For the earmuffs, spread a little frosting on the back of each Snow Puff cookie and affix 1 on each side of the snowman's head.

10. Using a spoon, lightly sprinkle the food glitter over the entire cake.

TEA PARTY!

It's all edible—the "tea" is a cupcake, the cup is made from frosting, and the handles are melted white chocolate. Just don't eat the teabag!

MAKES 24 STANDARD CUPCAKES

EQUIPMENT

Pans for 24 standard cupcakes

Paper cupcake liners

Toothpick

Wire cooling racks

Glass measuring cup

Waxed paper

Disposable decorating bag

Serrated knife

Small offset spatula

2 decorating bags, #12 round tip, and #3 round tip

24 teacup saucers

Skewer

24 paper "teabag" tags, 1 inch square, decorated by hand or computer

24 short pieces of string, each taped to a teabag tag

Small spoon

24 miniature taper candles (optional)

Serving tray

1. Preheat the oven to 350 °F. Fit 24 standard cupcake cups with paper liners. Fill them two-thirds full with batter. Bake the cupcakes until a toothpick inserted in the center comes out clean, 10 to 12 minutes. Cool the cupcakes in the pan on a cooling rack for 15 minutes and then turn out onto the rack to cool completely.

2. While the cupcakes are cooling, transfer ½ cup of the frosting to a glass measuring cup; tint it green (see page 12). Tint the remaining frosting yellow.

3. To make the handles, melt the chocolate wafers according to the manufacturer's directions. Photocopy the handle pattern (see page 103). Place a sheet of waxed paper on top of the pattern on a work surface. Transfer the melted chocolate to a disposable decorating bag; snip off the tip of the bag, leaving a small opening. Following the pattern, pipe a handle onto the waxed paper. Slide the paper over so you can pipe another handle. Repeat to make a handle for each cupcake. Let the handles harden while you decorate the cupcakes.

4. Remove the cooled cupcakes from their liners. Level the top of each (see page 10). Using an offset spatula, spread the yellow frosting over the top and sides of each cupcake. Fit a decorating bag with the #12 round tip; add the remaining yellow frosting to it. Pipe a rim along the top perimeter of each cupcake.

5. Fit a second decorating bag with the #3 round tip; add the green frosting to it. Referring to the photo, pipe a small vine spray onto each cupcake; affix a blue flower candy to it with a dab of frosting. →

101

If hot chocolate is more appealing than tea, skip the teabag tags and dot the cakes with mini marshmallows instead.

1 recipe Yellow Cake batter
(page 17)

1 recipe Creamy White Frosting
(page 21)

Green gel or paste food color

Yellow gel or paste food color

1 cup white chocolate melting
wafers (such as Wilton Candy Melts)

24 small blue candy flowers

1 cup light brown sugar

→ **6.** Lay out the saucers. One at a time, pipe some yellow frosting into each (enough to raise the cupcake a bit) and then place a cupcake on it. Attach a handle to each cupcake, adhering it with dabs of frosting. Pipe yellow beads around the bottom perimeter of each cupcake. For each, use even pressure to squeeze out a dab of frosting, then release the pressure and lift the tip.

7. Use a skewer to poke a small hole inside the rim of each teacup and poke a teabag string into each hole. For tea, spoon the brown sugar evenly over the top of each cupcake. Insert a candle in the center of each if you wish. Arrange the saucers with the cups of tea on a serving tray.

HANDLE PATTERN

ROCKIN' GUITAR

If this is a birthday cake, intersperse the candles with the candy decorations. This is a terrific cake for a budding guitarist or a rock-'n'-roll-themed party.

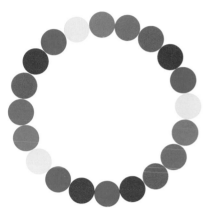

SERVES 12 TO 16
MAKES ONE 8-BY-19-INCH CAKE

EQUIPMENT

One 9-by-13-inch cake pan

Waxed or parchment paper

Toothpicks

Wire cooling racks

2 glass measuring cups

Cutting board

Ruler

Long serrated knife

Large platter or 10-by-20-inch cardboard base (see page 14), for serving

Small offset spatula

Decorating bag and #9 round tip

1. Preheat the oven to 350 °F. Lightly grease the bottom of the cake pan, then line it with waxed paper or parchment paper and grease and lightly flour the bottom and sides. Fill the prepared pan two-thirds full with batter. Bake the cake until a toothpick inserted in the center comes out clean, 35 to 40 minutes. Cool the cake completely in the pan on a cooling rack and then turn it out onto the rack.

2. While the cake is cooling, transfer ½ cup of frosting to each of 2 glass measuring cups. Tint 1 portion yellow and the other portion blue (see page 12). Tint the remaining 2 cups of frosting pink.

3. Place the cooled cake on a cutting board. Using a ruler and long serrated knife, cut across the cake 2 inches in from one 9-inch end to make the guitar neck; set it aside. Referring to the photo, use a toothpick to, prick the outline of the guitar body shape into the top of the remaining section. At its widest, the body is 8 inches across; in the middle it is 6½ inches across; it is 11 inches long. You can make a paper pattern first if you like (see page 10). Cut out the guitar body along the pricked outline; eat the scraps or discard them.

4. Arrange the guitar body and neck on the platter. Using an offset spatula, bond the neck to the body with a thin layer of the yellow frosting. Spread more yellow frosting over the top and sides of the neck. Using a clean spatula, spread the pink frosting over the top and sides of the body. →

1 tablespoon shortening

1 tablespoon flour

1 recipe Yellow Cake batter
(page 17)

1 recipe Creamy White Frosting
(page 21)

Yellow gel or paste food color

Blue gel or paste food color

Pink gel or paste food color

**One 4.25-ounce tube light blue
decorating icing**

6 gumdrops, assorted colors

1 chocolate wafer cookie

**One 4-inch-long piece Airhead Xtremes
Sweetly Sour Belts candy**

About 25 M&M's candies

About 5 Spree candies, assorted colors

**White cookie icing (available in
10-ounce bottle) or decorating icing,
for strings**

→ **5.** Fit the decorating bag with the round tip; add the blue frosting to the bag. Pipe a line of blue frosting all around the base of the assembled cake.

6. Decorate the neck using the light blue decorating icing: at the end, pipe a square with an X inside it as shown in the photo, then pipe frets across the neck at regular intervals. Place 3 gumdrops on each side of the neck at the top, adhering each with a dab of frosting.

7. Decorate the body: Place the wafer cookie in the middle, pressing it into the frosting. Center the Sweetly Sour Belts candy horizontally in the lower half of the body; press it into the frosting. Arrange the M&M's candies in a ring around the cookie and in a row on the horizontal band of candy; affix them to the candy with a dab of frosting. Press the Spree candies into the frosting below the horizontal candy.

8. Following the directions on the cookie icing bottle, pipe strings onto the guitar as shown.

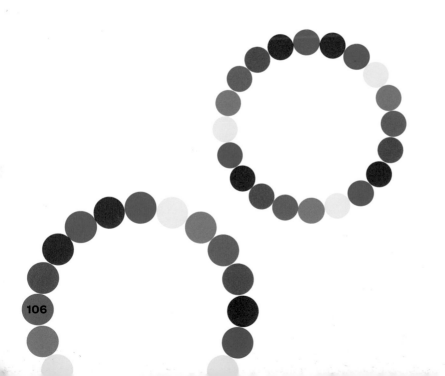

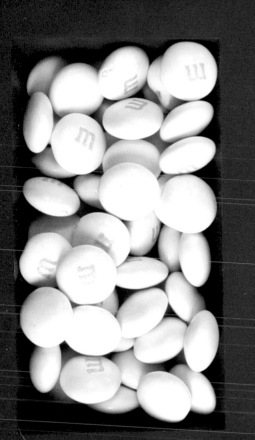

challenging

If you're like me, there are times when you want to pour all your creativity into one special project. That's where the cakes in this section come in. They may require a bit more patience and a bit more time than others in the book, but you don't need to be a professional to pull them off. The adorable Head's Up Giraffe (page 110), for instance, just requires a steady hand to fill in his spots with crushed cookie crumbs. The Princess Palace (page 122) will be easier to decorate if you're already comfortable piping icing through a pastry bag. I encourage you to read the recipes all the way through before you begin, so you can allot a realistic amount of time to creating one of these special cakes. And get ready for the oohs, aahs, and mountains of thanks you'll receive in the end.

projects

HEAD'S UP GIRAFFE

Who would think one nine-inch-square cake could grow sky-high? If your decorating experience is limited, practice piping and filling some spots on waxed paper before turning to the cake—you'll need a steady hand.

SERVES 6 TO 8
MAKES ONE 11-BY-21-INCH CAKE

EQUIPMENT

One 9-inch square cake pan

Waxed or parchment paper

Toothpick

Wire cooling racks

Cutting board

Ruler

Long serrated knife

Large platter or 12-by-21-inch cardboard base (see page 14), for serving

Small offset spatula

Decorating bag and #4 round tip

Very small spoon (such as the smallest in a set of measuring spoons)

Small, sharp knife

1 tablespoon shortening

1 tablespoon flour

1 recipe Marble Cake batter (page 18)

1 recipe Creamy White Frosting (page 21), tinted yellow

1 recipe Classic Icing Glaze (page 20), tinted brown

½ cup finely crushed chocolate wafer cookies or packaged Oreo Fine Crumbs

1 Junior Mints candy

1 sugar candy eye

5 chocolate-covered cookie rods

2 red chocolate-covered cherries (see Resources, page 128)

Fresh mint leaves

1. Preheat the oven to 350 °F. Lightly grease the bottom of the cake pan, then line it with waxed paper or parchment paper and grease and lightly flour the bottom and sides. Fill the prepared pan two-thirds full with batter. Bake the cake until a toothpick inserted in the center comes out clean, 30 to 35 minutes. If you wish, refer to the chart on page 15 to bake the surplus batter in a small pan or cupcake cups. Cool the cake completely in the pan on a cooling rack and then turn it out onto the rack.

2. Place the cooled cake on a cutting board. Using a ruler and serrated knife, cut the cake into the pieces shown in the cutting diagram (see page 112).

3. Arrange the cake pieces on the platter as shown in the layout diagram (see page 112). Cut 1 end of the tail so it fits against the body at a jaunty angle as shown. Using an offset spatula, bond adjacent pieces with a thin layer of frosting.

4. Spread the frosting over the top and sides of the cake. Using your fingers to mold it, fill out the contours of the giraffe with additional frosting.

5. Fit the decorating bag with the round tip; add the glaze to the bag. Referring to the photo, pipe outlines for the spots on the cake; make the outlines from ¾ to 1½ inches in diameter and use only the smaller size on the face. Leave an open area for the eye.

6. One at a time, fill the spots with the cookie crumbs: First pipe a thin layer of glaze into the spot. Then, using a very small spoon, carefully fill the spot with the crumbs. →

This giraffe's spots are filled with cookie crumbs. If some crumbs fall outside the piped spots, use a small paintbrush to carefully brush them off the cake.

→ **7.** Using a dab of glaze, attach the sugar candy eye to the Junior Mints candy. Affix the assembled eye to the cake with another dab of glaze.

8. Cut a 3-inch length from each of 2 chocolate-covered rods. Using a dab of glaze, affix a chocolate-covered cherry to the end of each 3-inch-long rod. Insert the rods into the top of the giraffe's head as shown in the photo.

9. Affixing them with glaze, arrange the 3 remaining chocolate rods end-to-end on the platter in front of the giraffe. Decorate with mint leaves as shown.

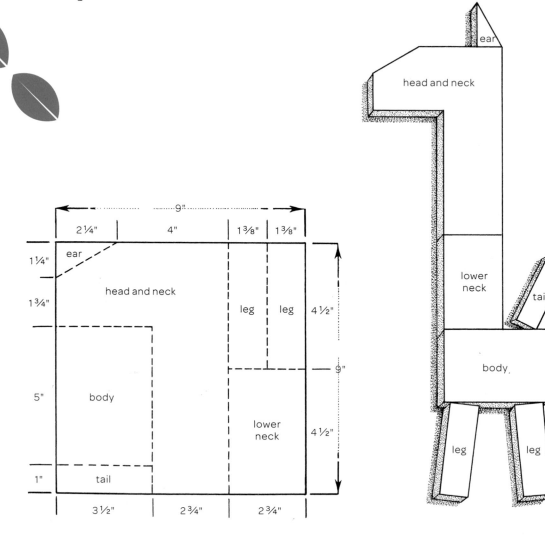

112

CUTTING DIAGRAM

LAYOUT DIAGRAM

GENIUS ROBOT

Calling all thinkers! There are so many shapes and colors of candy available—let your imagination be your guide when choosing decorations for this cake.

EQUIPMENT

One 9-by-13-inch cake pan

Waxed or parchment paper

Pan for 2 standard cupcakes

Paper cupcake liners

Toothpicks

Wire cooling racks

Cutting board

Ruler

Long serrated knife

Large platter or 14-by-19-inch cardboard base (see page 14), for serving

Small offset spatula

Decorating bag and #9 round tip

Small spoon

One 1½-by-2½-inch piece aluminum foil

7 silver mini muffin cup liners

1 recipe Marble Cake batter (page 18)

2 recipes Creamy White Frosting (page 21), tinted gray

One 10-ounce bottle white cookie icing

¼ cup large orange nonpareil sprinkles

2 large marshmallows, halved

3 silver dragées (6 mm size)

5 red candy wafers (such as Necco Wafers)

1 small red candy heart

About 25 pieces Chiclets gum, assorted colors (including 6 white, for teeth and eyes)

2 white candy wafers (such as Necco Wafers)

About 10 small red round candies (such as SweeTarts)

2 lollipops

1. Preheat the oven to 350 °F. Lightly grease the bottom of the cake pan, then line it with waxed paper or parchment paper and grease and lightly flour the bottom and sides. Fit the cupcake cups with paper liners. Fill the cupcake cups two-thirds full, then spread the remaining batter in the rectangular pan. Bake until a toothpick inserted in the center comes out clean, 10 to 12 minutes for the cupcakes, and 30 to 40 minutes for the rectangular pan. Cool the cake completely in the pan on a cooling rack and then turn it out onto the rack. Cool the cupcakes in the pan on a cooling rack for 15 minutes and then turn out onto the rack to cool completely.

2. Place the cooled cake on a cutting board. Using a ruler and serrated knife, cut the cake into the pieces shown in the cutting diagram (see page 115). Level the top of each cupcake (see page 10) and, referring to the photo, cut an arc out of each so it will resemble a wrench when attached to the robot's arm.

3. Arrange the cake pieces on the platter as shown in the layout diagram (see page 115). Cut 1 end of each arm as shown. Using an offset spatula, bond adjacent pieces with a thin layer of frosting. Eat the scraps or discard them.

4. Set aside ¾ cup of frosting. Spread the remaining frosting over the top and sides of the cake. Fit the decorating bag with the round tip; add the reserved frosting to the bag. Pipe a line of frosting all around the base of the assembled cake. →

113

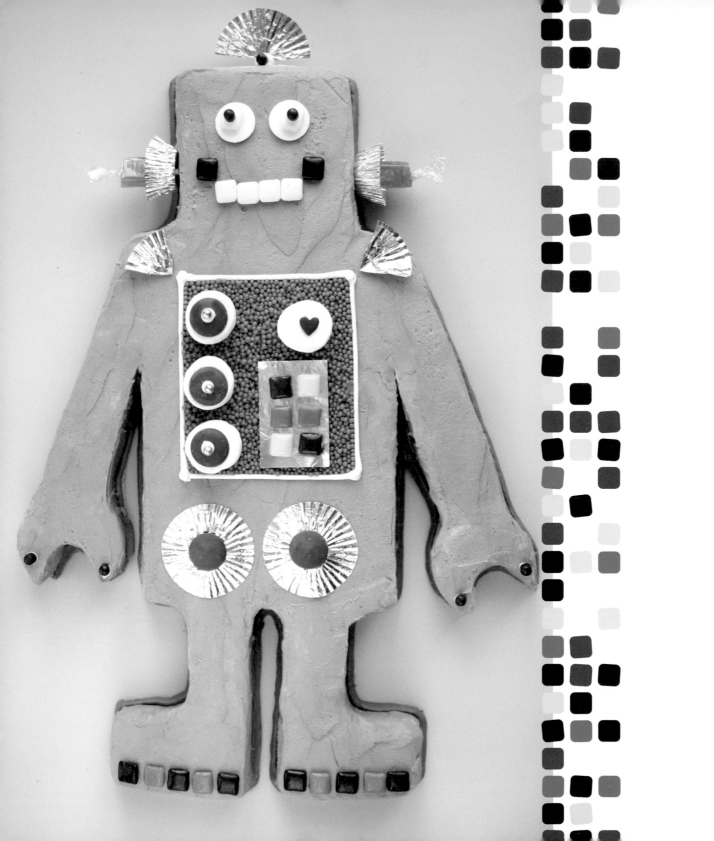

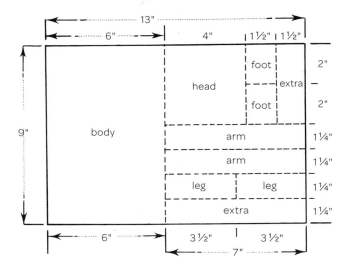

		foot			2"
	head	extra			
		foot			2"
body	arm				1¼"
	arm				1¼"
	leg	leg			1¼"
	extra				1¼"

13" · 6" · 4" · 1½" · 1½"
9" · 6" · 3½" · 3½" · 7"

CUTTING DIAGRAM

→ **5.** Decorate the chest: Referring to the photo, use the cookie icing to outline a 5-by-7-inch rectangle on the robot's chest. Spoon the nonpareils inside the rectangle, filling it completely. Line up 3 marshmallow halves inside the left side of the rectangle; affix each with a dab of cookie icing. Using a dab of the cookie icing, affix a dragée to the center of each of 3 red candy wafers, then affix the wafers to the top of the marshmallows. Affix the remaining marshmallow half inside the upper right corner of the rectangle. Affix the red candy heart to it with a dab of icing. Affix the aluminum foil with icing in the rectangle as shown. Affix assorted Chiclets to it with dabs of icing.

6. Arrange the face: Referring to the photo and adhering each with a dab of cookie icing, arrange 4 white Chiclets for the teeth and add another Chiclet at each end as shown. For each eye, top a white candy wafer with a white Chiclet and then a small red candy, adhering with dabs of icing. Affix the eyes on top of the cake.

7. Flatten 2 of the silver muffin liners. Affix them with dabs of icing below the orange rectangle. Affix a red candy wafer to the center of each. Flatten 2 more silver liners and fold each into quarters; affix 1 outside each upper corner of the orange rectangle. Flatten another silver liner and fold it in half. Use a dab of icing to affix it to a toothpick; insert it in the cake side at the top of the head. Affix a small red candy to it as shown. Also affix a small red candy to each robot fingertip.

8. Poke a hole in the center of each remaining silver liner. For each ear, insert the stick of a lollipop through the hole in a liner and then into the side of the cake at the side of the head. Remove the lollipops and silver liner head ornament before cutting the cake.

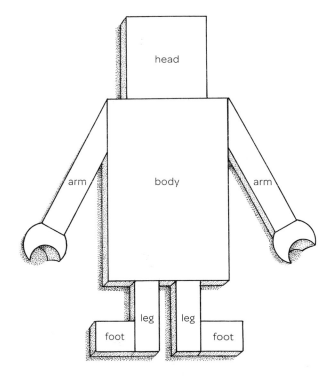

LAYOUT DIAGRAM

Arrange the dinosaur so the head is straight in front of the body if you like.

DELICIOUS DINOSAUR

Fossilization is out of the question for this guy—he'll never last that long. Choose whatever color frosting, fruit slices, and candy dots you like.

SERVES 11 TO 15
MAKES ONE 6-BY-16-BY-3½-INCH CAKE

EQUIPMENT

One 6-inch round cake pan

One 9-inch round cake pan

Waxed or parchment paper

Toothpick

Wire cooling racks

Cutting board

Long serrated knife

Small offset spatula

Large platter or 17-by-17-inch cardboard base (see page 14), for serving

Decorating bag and #1A round tip

2 tablespoons shortening

2 tablespoons flour

1 recipe Marble Cake batter (page 18)

2 recipes Creamy White Frosting (page 21), tinted yellow

2 red Spree candies

About 15 green half-round candy fruit slices

About 75 small blue candy dots (such as Necco Wafers Old Fashioned Candy Buttons)

One 4.25-ounce tube black decorating icing

2 white candy wafers (such as Necco Wafers)

1. Preheat the oven to 350 °F. Lightly grease the bottom of each cake pan, then line it with waxed paper or parchment paper and grease and lightly flour the bottom and sides. Fill the prepared pans two-thirds full with batter. Bake until a toothpick inserted in the center comes out clean, 20 to 25 minutes for the 6-inch pan, and 30 to 35 minutes for the 9-inch pan. If you wish, refer to the chart on page 15 to bake the surplus batter in a small pan or as cupcakes. Cool the cakes completely in the pans on cooling racks and then turn them out onto the racks.

2. Place the cooled cakes on a cutting board. Using the serrated knife, cut each in half vertically, as shown in the cutting diagram (see page 118). Using an offset spatula, spread frosting over the top of one 6-inch half-round and one 9-inch half-round; stack the matching halves on top of each.

3. To shape the head, turn the smaller cake so the curved edge faces away from you. At the left end of the arc, starting about 1½ inches above the straight edge, cut away a wide pie-shaped wedge about 1½ inches on each straight side as shown in the assembly and cutting diagram (see page 118). Turn the cake so the curved face is up; the cutout section shapes the jaw and forehead and the seam between the cake layers runs from chin to nape.

4. Transfer the larger cake to 1 end of the platter, turning it so the curved face is up; this is the body. Referring to the photo, place the head on the platter at an angle to the body. Set aside 2 cups of frosting. Using the spatula, spread the remaining frosting over all of the surfaces of each cake. →

→ **5.** Fit the decorating bag with the round tip; add the reserved frosting to the bag. Refer to the photo as you refine the shape: Pipe out some frosting between the head and body to create a neck; mold it with your fingers. (It helps to dip your fingers in cornstarch when molding frosting, to keep it from sticking.) Pipe extra frosting around the head where it meets the platter and mold with your fingers so the base is wider than the top of the head as shown. Pipe some frosting to create the tail and each leg, molding each as shown. For the nostrils, pipe 2 bumps of frosting on top of the jaw; then press a red candy into each.

6. Arrange 2 rows of 6 fruit slices along the top of the back as shown; place the 2 remaining slices on the tail. Add the candy dots to the head and body.

7. With the black decorating icing, pipe a line around the jaw as shown for the mouth. For eyes, pipe a large dot onto each white candy wafer, then press each into the face as shown.

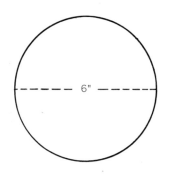

6"

CUTTING DIAGRAM

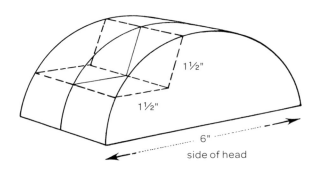

1½"

1½"

6"

side of head

ASSEMBLY AND CUTTING DIAGRAM

PICKUP TRUCK

Let your child choose the cargo for the back of this truck— you could use Tootsie Rolls, gumdrops, chocolate rocks, or go with the wafer cookie "logs" shown in the photo.

SERVES 10 TO 12
MAKES ONE 6-BY-8-BY-3 ½-INCH CAKE

EQUIPMENT

Two 4 ½-by-8 ½-by-2 ½-inch loaf pans

Waxed or parchment paper

Toothpicks

Wire cooling racks

2 glass measuring cups

Long serrated knife

Platter or 9-by-9-inch cardboard base (see page 14), for serving

Small offset spatula

3 decorating bags

1 or 2 #9 round tips, #4 round tip

Small serrated knife

Small spoon

1. Preheat the oven to 350 °F. Lightly grease the bottom of each cake pan, then line it with waxed paper or parchment paper and grease and lightly flour the bottom and sides. Referring to the package directions, prepare the batter for the cake. Divide the batter between the pans. Bake the cakes until a toothpick inserted in the center comes out clean, 25 to 30 minutes. Cool the cakes completely in the pans on cooling racks and then turn them out onto the racks.

2. While the cakes are cooling, spoon ¼ cup of the frosting into a glass measuring cup; tint it gray (see page 12). Spoon another ½ cup frosting into another glass measuring cup; set aside. Tint the remainder of the frosting blue.

3. Level the top of each cooled cake (see page 10). Place 1 cake on the serving platter to be the truck body. To make the cab, use the serrated knife to cut a 3-inch-deep piece off the second cake. Refer-ring to the photo, place the piece just cut on top of the truck body, setting it about 2 inches from 1 end. Using an offset spatula, bond the cab to the truck body with a thin layer of blue frosting. Eat the remainder of the cake or discard it.

4. Fit a decorating bag with the #9 round tip; add the gray frosting to the bag. On each end of the truck body, pipe a line of gray frosting to be a bumper as shown in the photo on page 120. →

To serve more people, perch the truck on top of a larger rectangular cake—decorate this base to look like a meadow or a highway.

2 tablespoons shortening

2 tablespoons flour

One 18.25-ounce chocolate cake mix

One 1-pound can white frosting

Gray gel or paste food color

Blue gel or paste food color

4 chocolate-covered sandwich cookies

One 4.25-ounce tube white decorating icing

One 4.25-ounce tube black decorating icing

2 round yellow SweeTart candies

About 5 pieces black coated-licorice candy (such as Good & Plenty)

About 5 pieces white coated-licorice candy (such as Good & Plenty)

About 5 chocolate-covered rectangular wafer cookies

Gold sanding sugar, for dusting

→ **5.** Fit a second decorating bag with the #4 round tip; add the white frosting to the bag. Pipe the outline of a window on each side of the cab; pipe more frosting inside each outline, spreading with a clean spatula to fill in the window.

6. Fit a third decorating bag with another #9 round tip (or wash and dry the first tip); add the blue frosting to the bag. Carefully pipe around each bumper and window, then pipe and spread blue frosting over the rest of the truck.

7. Using a dab of blue frosting to adhere each, place 2 sandwich cookies on each side of the truck for wheels. Pipe some blue frosting on top of each wheel as shown. With the tube of white decorating icing, pipe spokes onto each wheel.

8. Referring to the photo, add details with the black decorating icing: Outline each window, adding a rear-view mirror to the side doors and wipers to the windshield; outline the hood and each door; pipe along the bottom edge on the front, back, and sides between the wheels; and pipe a dot in the center of each wheel.

9. For headlights, press the SweeTart candies into the frosting on the front of the truck above the bumper. For the grille, press the black licorice candies between the headlights. For parking lights, press a white licorice candy onto the front bumper below each headlight; press corresponding parking lights onto the back bumper.

10. To make logs for the back of the truck, use a small serrated knife to cut the wafer cookies in half lengthwise. Sprinkle the sanding sugar over the back of the truck with a small spoon. Arrange the logs on top. Sprinkle a bit of sanding sugar on the serving platter too if you like.

PRINCESS PALACE

For the true princess in your life—this is a challenging confection that experienced decorators will love to make. Be sure to have six decorating bags on hand, one for each of the six tips.

SERVES 16 TO 20
MAKES ONE 8-BY-9-INCH CAKE

EQUIPMENT

Two 6-inch round cake pans

Two 9-inch round cake pans

Waxed or parchment paper

Toothpicks

Wire cooling racks

One 6-inch diameter cardboard base

One 9-inch diameter cardboard base

2 glass measuring cups

Small offset spatula

Cake plate or 10-inch cardboard base (see page 14), for serving

3 decorating bags with coupler assemblies (see page 9)

#16 star tip, #3 round tip, #47 basket weave tip, #12 round tip, #30 star tip

Paper banner with message (optional)

Miniature taper candles (optional)

3 to 4 tablespoons shortening

3 to 4 tablespoons flour

2 recipes Yellow Cake batter (page 17)

2 recipes Creamy White Frosting (page 21)

Pink gel or paste food color

Purple gel or paste food color

Pastel mini marshmallows, for crenellations

Pink sugar pearls, for star centers

4 small pink sugar heart candies

Eight 1-inch sugar heart candies

1. Preheat the oven to 350 °F. Lightly grease the bottom of each cake pan, then line it with waxed paper or parchment paper and grease and lightly flour the bottom and sides. Fill the prepared pans two-thirds full with batter. Bake the 6-inch cakes until a toothpick inserted in the center comes out clean, 20 to 25 minutes. Then bake the 9-inch cakes until a toothpick inserted in the center comes out clean, 30 to 35 minutes. If you wish, refer to the chart on page 15 to bake the surplus batter in a small pan or as cupcakes. Cool the cakes completely in the pans on cooling racks and then turn them out onto the racks. Place one of each size cake onto a cardboard base.

2. While the cakes are cooling, transfer ½ cup frosting to each of 2 glass measuring cups. Tint the remaining 5 cups frosting light pink. Tint 1 of the ½-cup portions light purple. Leave the other one white.

3. Using an offset spatula, spread pink frosting over the top of 1 of each size cake; top each with the remaining same-size cake. Transfer each stack to the corresponding cardboard base. Set aside 1 cup of the pink frosting. Spread the remaining pink frosting over the top and sides of each cake.

4. Transfer the 9-inch cake on its cardboard base to the center of the serving plate. Center the 6-inch cake, on its base, on top of it.

5. Fit a decorating bag with the #16 star tip; add the reserved pink frosting to the bag. Referring to the photo, pipe shells around the top perimeter of each tier: For each, hold the bag at a 45-degree angle to the cake and moving the tip slightly, use even pressure to squeeze out the shell shape, then raise →

Place windows and candy hearts all around the castle so it looks pretty from any angle.

happy birthday, lily

→ the tip and decrease the pressure to make a point; stop the pressure and, leaving room for a mini marshmallow, reposition the tip for the next shell. Press mini marshmallows into the frosting between the shells.

6. Using the same tip, pipe a star border around the base of the top tier: For each star, hold the bag straight up with the tip against the cake; squeeze the bag, keeping the tip in the frosting until the star forms; stop the pressure and reposition the tip for the next star.

7. Fit a second decorating bag with a #3 round tip; add the white frosting to the bag. Referring to the photo, pipe squiggly lines of varying lengths on the side of the top tier, drawing them down from the shell border. With the pink frosting and the star tip, add individual stars randomly between and below the squiggly lines; lightly press a pink sugar pearl into the center of each star.

8. Make the door and windows: Referring to the photo, use a toothpick to prick the outline of the door and windows on the frosting. The door is 2 inches wide and 3 inches tall; the windows are 7/8 inch wide and 1¾ inches tall (you can make paper patterns for them first if you like).

9. Fit a third decorating bag with another #3 round tip (or wash and dry the first one); add the purple frosting to the bag. Pipe a line of frosting along each pricked outline. Then pipe more frosting inside each shape, spreading to fill with a clean spatula. Exchange the round tip for the basket weave tip, and cover the door with vertical planks, drawing each from bottom to top. Switching back to the round tip, pipe beads around the door: For each, use even pressure to squeeze out a small amount of frosting, then release the pressure and lift the tip. Pipe a vertical line in the center of the door and pipe 2 beads for doorknobs. Also pipe

a line for each arched window frame and beads for each windowsill. Affix a small candy heart to each window with a dab of frosting.

10. Fit the decorating bag holding pink frosting with a #12 round tip. Pipe a bead border around the bottom of the cake; pipe another bead border right above the first.

11. Make the towers: Change to a #30 star tip. Referring to the photo, pipe 3 conical towers on top of the cake: For each, first pipe a circle on the cake top and then, without stopping, lift the tip and pipe a spiral of decreasing rounds until the cone is about 2 ½ inches tall. Stop the pressure and end the cone with a peak. Place a 1-inch sugar heart in the top of each tower.

12. Using a dab of frosting, affix each remaining 1-inch sugar heart between the door and a window. Add the banner and candles if you wish.

ROCKET TO THE MOON

Serve this to celebrate July 4th, or have a blast choosing candies that honor a personal space fantasy. If you don't have the right small cake pans, bake in larger pans and then cut the layers to size.

SERVES 22 TO 30
MAKES ONE 11-BY-15-INCH CAKE

EQUIPMENT

Two 6-inch round cake pans

Three 5-inch round cake pans

Two 4-inch round cake pans

One 8-inch square cake pan

Waxed or parchment paper

Toothpicks

Wire cooling racks

Cutting board

Ruler

Long serrated knife

One 6-inch cardboard cake base

One 5-inch cardboard cake base

One 4-inch cardboard cake base

Small offset spatula

6 plastic drinking straws

Large plate or 8-inch cardboard base (see page 14), for serving

4 flag picks

Shortening, as needed

Flour, as needed

3 recipes Yellow Cake batter (page 17)

2 recipes Creamy White Frosting (page 21)

1 waffle ice cream cone

Coated licorice candies (red, white, and black), for decoration

Jelly beans (red, white, and blue), for decoration

6 to 8 red jelly rings

6 to 8 blue gumballs

1. Preheat the oven to 350 °F. Lightly grease the bottom of each cake pan, then line it with waxed paper or parchment paper and grease and lightly flour the bottom and sides. Fill each prepared pan two-thirds full with batter. Working in batches so that the oven isn't too full to heat evenly, bake the round cakes until a toothpick inserted in the center comes out clean, 20 to 30 minutes, checking early for doneness; bake the square cake for 30 to 35 minutes. There will be quite a bit of extra batter; refer to the chart on page 15 to bake it in another pan or in cupcake cups. Cool the cakes completely in the pans on cooling racks and then turn them out onto the racks.

2. Place the cooled square cake on a cutting board. For the rocket fins, measure to find the midpoint of each edge and mark by pricking with a toothpick. Using the serrated knife and cutting from mark to mark on adjacent edges, cut off each corner of the cake. Set aside 3 corners for the fins; reserve 1 corner and the center square for another purpose.

3. Place one cake of each size on a cardboard base. Using an offset spatula, frost the tops of all of the round cakes; stack each of the matching cakes.

4. To provide support for the upper sections of the rocket, insert 3 straws vertically into the 6-inch round layered cake; place them about 1 inch inside the perimeter, space them at equal intervals, and push each straw all the way down so it rests on the cardboard base. Snip the straws flush with the cake top. Repeat to insert 3 straws into the 5-inch round layered cake. →

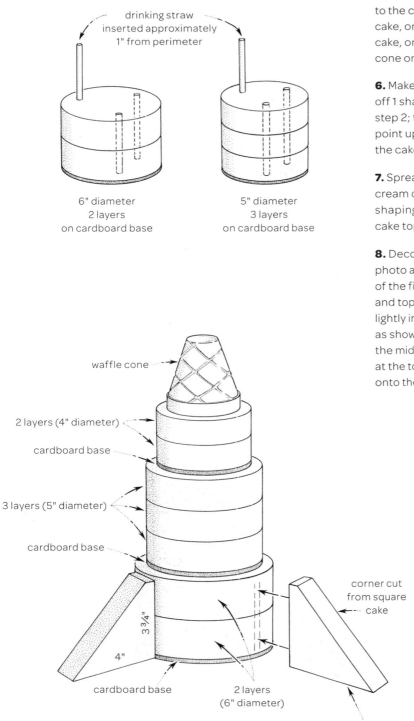

drinking straw
inserted approximately
1" from perimeter

6" diameter
2 layers
on cardboard base

5" diameter
3 layers
on cardboard base

waffle cone

2 layers (4" diameter)

cardboard base

3 layers (5" diameter)

cardboard base

3 3/4"

4"

corner cut
from square
cake

cardboard base

2 layers
(6" diameter)

3 fins are spaced around cake

→ **5.** Transfer the 6-inch cake on its cardboard base to the center of the serving plate. Center the 5-inch cake, on its base, on top of it. Center the 4-inch cake, on its base, on top of that. Invert the ice cream cone on top of the stacked cakes.

6. Make the fins: Referring to the photo, cut ¼ inch off 1 sharp point of each corner triangle made in step 2; then, spacing them evenly with the blunted point up, position each against the bottom tier of the cake. Secure each with a thin layer of frosting.

7. Spread frosting over the entire cake and the ice cream cone. Use extra frosting around the cone, shaping it so it blends with the perimeter of the cake top.

8. Decorate the rocket with the candies: Refer to the photo and place the licorice pieces along the edges of the fins and tiers, at the bottom of the middle and top tiers, and also up the cone; press the pieces lightly into the frosting. Add the jelly beans in stripes as shown. Add the jelly rings and gumballs around the middle tier. Insert a flag pick in each fin and also at the top of the rocket. Sprinkle more jelly beans onto the plate.

Resources

BAKING AND DECORATING SUPPLIES

While the baking aisle in most grocery stores offers cake mixes, ready-made frosting, and basic cake decorating supplies, mass-market craft stores and discount department stores have entire aisles dedicated to the art of cake making and decorating. Visit them in person or online to find lots of choices for cake pans, spatulas, decorating bags and tips, paste and gel food color, ready-made frosting and decorating icing, colored sugars and all sorts of sprinkles, and fun decorations like sugar candy eyes and flowers. Many of these stores also carry a good assortment of useful snack candies as well as birthday candles.

Also check out specialty cake creators in your area. Many offer classes and sell supplies and bake to order. The one near me in New Hampshire, Chandler's Cake and Candy Supplies (www.chandlerscake.com and www.chandlerscakeandcandy.com), is invaluable to us.

The following vendors offer diverse supplies online as well as in conventional stores:

A.C. Moore www.acmoore.com

Jo-Ann Fabrics www.joann.com

Michael's www.michaels.com

Target www.target.com

Wal-Mart www.walmart.com

Wilton www.wilton.com

CANDIES, NUTS, CARAMEL POPCORN

There are many online vendors of classic and retro candies and some that specialize in gourmet sweets that make good decorations too. Two we find useful:

Harry and David www.harryanddavid.com

Yummies Candy and Nuts www.yummies.com

SERVING PLATTERS, CANDLES, AND OTHER PARTY SUPPLIES

Visit these vendors online to order directly or find a nearby store:

Crate & Barrel www.crateandbarrel.com

Hallmark www.hallmark.com

Home Goods www.homegoods.com

iparty www.iparty.com

Sur la Table www.surlatable.com

Williams-Sonoma www.williams-sonoma.com

Index